Maria and Lola
Stories of Survival

As told to Gregoria Boursinos
And written by
Carol Freeman Gordon and Gregoria Boursinos

A Publication of JewishGen
Edmond J. Safra Plaza, 36 Battery Place, New York, NY 10280
646.494.2972 | info@JewishGen.org | www.jewishgen.org

JewishGen is the Genealogical Research Division of the
Museum of Jewish Heritage – A Living Memorial to the
Holocaust

Maria and Lola: Stories of Survival

Copyright © 2025 by Carol Freeman Gordon. All rights reserved.
Published by JewishGen
First Printing: August 2025, Av 5785

Author: Carol Freeman Gordon and Gregoria Boursinos

Cover Design: Rachel Kolokoff Hopper

This book may not be reproduced, in whole or in part, including illustrations in any form (beyond that copying permitted by Sections 107 and 108 of the U.S. Copyright Law and except by reviewers for public press), without written permission from the copyright holder.

JewishGen is not responsible for inaccuracies or omissions in the original work and makes no representations regarding its accuracy.

Library of Congress Control Number (LCCN): 2025942069

ISBN: 978-1-962054-32-4 (softcover: 320 pages, alk. paper)

About JewishGen.org

JewishGen, is a Genealogical Research Division of the Museum of Jewish Heritage - A Living Memorial to the Holocaust, serves as the global home for Jewish genealogy.

Featuring unparalleled access to 30+ million records, it offers unique search tools, along with opportunities for researchers to connect with others who share similar interests. Award winning resources such as the Family Finder, Discussion Groups, and ViewMate, are relied upon by thousands each day.

In addition, JewishGen's extensive informational, educational and historical offerings, such as the Jewish Communities Database, Yizkor Book translations, InfoFiles, Family Tree of the Jewish People, and KehilaLinks, provide critical insights, first-hand accounts, and context about Jewish communal and familial life throughout the world.

Offered as a free resource, JewishGen.org has facilitated thousands of family connections and success stories, and is currently engaged in an intensive expansion effort that will bring many more records, tools, and resources to its collections.

Please visit https://www.jewishgen.org/ to learn more.

Vice President for JewishGen: Avraham Groll

About JewishGen Press

JewishGen Press (formerly the Yizkor Books-in-Print Project) is the publishing division of JewishGen.org, and provides a venue for the publication of non-fiction books pertaining to Jewish genealogy, history, culture, and heritage.

In addition to the Yizkor Book category, publications in the Other Non-Fiction category include Shoah memoirs and research, genealogical research, collections of genealogical and historical materials, biographies, diaries and letters, studies of Jewish experience and cultural life in the past, academic theses, and other books of interest to the Jewish community.

Please visit https://www.jewishgen.org/Yizkor/ybip.html to learn more.

Director of JewishGen Press: Joel Alpert
Managing Editor - Peter Harris
Publications Manager - Susan Rosin

Cover Photo Credits

Cover designed by Rachel Kolokoff Hopper

Front Cover:
Salonica 1942 – Lola (left) and Maria (right), page 134
Background Photos:
- *Maria,* page 4
- *Salonica 1938 – Israel Seror,* page 130
- *Salonica 1937 – Maria,* page 130
- *Salonica 1939 - Maria on holiday,* page 131
- *Salonica 1940 - Maria (left) and Lola (right),* page 132
- *Salonica 1945 - Maria after liberation,* page 136
- *Salonica circa late 1946 – Maria and her beau, George Curtis,* page 138
- *Belgium 1946 – Lola,* page 139
- *Salonica 1947 – Maria and George wedding day. Maria's friend Stella and her husband (back Left). Stella's two daughters are the bridesmaids,* page 140

Front and Back Cover Color Background and Texture:
Rachel Kolokoff Hopper
Front and Back Cover Background Collage:
Rachel Kolokoff Hopper

MARIA & LOLA:

Stories of Survival

As told to Gregoria Boursinos

And written by

Carol Freeman Gordon and Gregoria Boursinos

FOREWORD

This book recounts the stories of two Jewish Sephardic Greek sisters – Maria and Lola Seror – sole Survivors of the Holocaust of their entire family. Maria was born on the 21st March 1923 and Lola was born on the 16th May 1926. They lived in Salonica (later known as Thessaloniki).

Maria's name was Rachel until she went into hiding during the Nazi occupation of Greece and the persecution of the Jews. Maria decided to keep her new name as she transitioned into her new life after the war.

Maria survived in hiding and Lola survived incarceration in concentration camps and death marches. The two sisters were joyfully reunited in Melbourne, Australia some years after the war.

Their remarkable journeys of survival were told to Gregoria Boursinos and were written by Carol Freeman Gordon and Gregoria Boursinos.

Memory is very personal and circumstantial and this is evidenced by the recollections of the two sisters. Their stories were recorded more than seventy years after the fact and therefore it is not surprising that small details may differ in their memory of certain events.

What can never be forgotten is the horror and trauma of their experiences during the Holocaust.

Their wish in sharing their stories is that the reader becomes the witness and helps to ensure that their stories will never be forgotten.

This book is dedicated to the Seror family of Thessaloniki who were murdered during the Holocaust and to all the Jews of Greece who met the same tragic fate.

BOOK ONE

MARIA'S STORY

CHAPTER ONE

The Hacienda

Rachel Seror's home was in a hacienda[1] which was located in the centre of the city of Salonica in Greece at 46 Aphroditis Street. The second oldest of five children, she was born there on the 21st March 1923, as her older brother had been, and all her siblings after her. It was a beautiful home which had been part of her mother's dowry. The front entrance had decorative iron double doors with a Venetian lion's head handle.

There were five houses inside the hacienda - one on either side and three at the back behind the courtyard. All of the families living in the hacienda were related. As was typical of a hacienda, there was a big old fashioned kitchen on the ground floor which the five families shared. Each family also had their own small kitchen for every-day meals. It was a two hundred year old building when Rachel was born and over the years it had been constantly updated. Rachel's maternal grandmother's ancestors had built the hacienda in the 18th Century after having lived in Salonica for close to a hundred years. They had come to Greece in 1492 as penniless Jewish refugees who fled Toledo, Spain during the Inquisition. Over time they established themselves in Salonica and once the family had enough money, their first priority was to build a hacienda, as was the tradition back in Spain. Despite being outcast during the Spanish Inquisition, they

---

[1] *Spanish* A large estate with dwellings.

still felt Spanish at heart. After four hundred years in Greece they identified themselves as Greek-Spaniards of the Jewish faith.

Rachel's father's name was Israel and her mother's name was Emma. Her father, a tall sturdy man, owned a tinsmith factory which was located four blocks from the hacienda. He had special machinery that made different types of tins for jam, halva, olive oil and other produce. He supplied many businesses with these tins. He worked there with his first cousin. When his oldest child and only son Moishe came of age, he began working in the family business as well. Father and son not only worked together but they also enjoyed fishing together and played soccer every Sunday with other family members.

Rachel also had three younger sisters, Lola, Mathilde and Arietta. At home the family spoke Ladino[2] and Greek. The parents also spoke French as they had attended a French speaking school in Salonica in the early 1900s. When they didn't want the children to understand what they were saying, they spoke in French. There were many Saturday afternoons when Rachel could hear, from her bedroom window, her mother chatting away in French with their neighbours as they sat eating pumpkin seeds.

They were a happy family with all the things that go with it. As a young girl Rachel was a tomboy, she was literally not afraid of anything. There were many things from her childhood that Rachel would never forget. One

---

[2] A nearly extinct Romance language descended from medieval Spanish, spoken by the Jews in the Balkans.

day at the age of twelve, Rachel was waiting at the hacienda's gates for her father to come home from work. Her mother, who was inside the hacienda, saw her and told her to come in and close the front gate but Rachel didn't listen. Her mother came over to close the gates and at that moment they heard a hissing sound. They both looked up and saw a huge snake lying along the top of the gate. Mother grabbed Rachel's arm and ran inside. Rachel was not afraid so she picked up a bowl of sugar and went back to the hacienda's gate where she threw some sugar at the snake and it slithered away. This was a superstition that her ancestors brought with them from Spain and it seemed to work every time.

Around the same time, Rachel's favourite pastime was to go from roof to roof around the neighbourhood. On one such outing, she fell through a roof which had a skylight. She fell into her neighbour's kitchen and they helped her up but scolded her at the same time. Her parents told her that she was lucky to only receive a scar on her face and they grounded her for the rest of the summer. It was during this time when Rachel began to do embroidery. She was stuck indoors all day and by the end of the summer she had completed an entire piece. Her mother, who was also excellent at embroidery, put her to work to begin filling up her trousseau for her dowry, which was something that every Jewish girl of Salonica had. She embroidered a multitude of pillow cases and tablecloths, large and small.

The hacienda saw many religious occasions and parties. Rachel's parents were more traditional than religious. The family celebrated all the *Yamim*

Tovim[3] and it was only during these occasions that her father attended the *sinagoga*[4].

Rachel's mother always kept *Shabbos.*[5] On Friday evening the candles were always on the dining room table next to a jug of *Kosher*[6] wine and two loaves of *challah*[7] bread that were home made by her mother. Her mother would put on a lace headscarf and light the candles. She then covered her eyes with her hands before reciting the blessing. There was no cooking done during the Sabbath in adherence with the laws of the Sabbath which prohibit manual labour. They cooked a double quantity of food on Friday during the day and on Saturday, their non-Jewish neighbour's daughter would come to their house and light up the stove. The family would then warm up the food as they needed it. Rachel recalls one Friday night, as the family was about to begin their Sabbath meal, there was a knock on the door. Rachel's father answered the door to find a beggar standing there pleading for a slice of bread with a drizzle of olive oil. Instead of just giving him a piece of bread and sending him on his way, Rachel's father invited him in and they shared their Sabbath meal with a complete stranger. Her family was so accepting that they did not care if he was Jewish or not. They soon realised that he was a Christian as he made the sign of the cross before taking his first bite.

---

[3] *Hebrew* Jewish holidays, also known as Jewish festivals.
[4] *Ladino* A Jewish Synagogue.
[5] *Hebrew* The Sabbath.
[6] *Hebrew* Food that is fit for consumption according to Jewish law.
[7] A special Jewish braided bread eaten on Sabbath and Jewish Holidays.

Passover[8] was an important Jewish holiday in their household. The three families in the hacienda would sit together for the Seder[9] meal. Rachel's family were Sephardic[10] Jews and their Passover meal consisted of traditional dishes that their ancestors had eaten for centuries. Fish was the centrepiece for both courses.

Rachel's father would often say "Passover is not Passover without fish." During this festival, Mother's voice could be heard echoing throughout the house.

"Rachel, take out the cazuela[11], it needs to be koshered."[12]

Rachel always helped with the Passover preparations and it was one of her favourite times of the year. She especially loved preparing the soup and she always put in extra saffron, not just for flavour but for colour as well. For the main course, Rachel's mother prepared the most sumptuous dish with red and green peppers, potatoes and onions. She would bake these vegetables together with five bream fish. It was a Spanish style dish that had passed down from generation to generation.

On this night there was always plenty of red kosher wine and it was one night when the children were allowed to drink. The one thing their mother

---

[8] The major Jewish spring festival which commemorates the liberation of the Israelites from Egyptian slavery, lasting eight days.
[9] A Jewish ritual service and ceremonial dinner for the first two nights of Passover.
[10] Descendants of the Jews who lived in Spain and Portugal during the Middle Ages until the 15th and 16th centuries.
[11] *Spanish* A cooking pot.
[12] All cooking vessels are made kosher through an intricate process that is required by Jewish law.

didn't make was the matzah[13]. Every year the Seror family bought ten huge, round matzah sheets from their local Jewish bakery. Rachel's mother had a big container where she kept the matzah. During the eight days of Passover they would break off as much matzah as they needed and this would last them for the entire holiday. Another dish that Rachel looked forward to during Passover was matzah de vino[14]. This was a thick, round unleavened bread that was made with wine, olive oil, onions, and garlic. This was the perfect accompaniment to eat with the charoset[15], which Rachel prepared with her mother. The charoset was very sweet with plenty of dates, apples and walnuts mixed with honey, red wine and a lot of cinnamon and nutmeg.

For all the Yom Tov[16] holidays, the Seror children wore their best clothes. As Rachel was the oldest girl she always received brand new clothes for the Holidays and her sister Lola wore the hand-me-downs.

As wonderful as all the Holidays were, Rachel's favourite was Purim[17], which usually coincided with Apokries[18]. For two to three weeks prior to

---

[13] Unleavened flatbread, traditionally eaten by Jews during Passover.
[14] *Spanish and Italian* Wine.
[15] A sticky, sweet symbolic food that Jews eat during their Passover meal every year.
[16] A phrase describing a religious holiday. Literally means 'Good Day'.
[17] A Jewish holiday in which Jews commemorate being saved from persecution in the ancient Persian Empire.
[18] 'Apokries' is Carnival time which takes place during the last three weeks before Lent.

'Clean Monday'[19], Salonica was one big carnival. With Purim being celebrated by the Jewish community at the same time, there were multiple parties to pick and choose from. Two or three times during that week, all of the five families living in the hacienda dressed up in their carnival clothes and eye masks. Their house had a reputation for holding the best party in the neighbourhood. Behind the kitchen was a huge courtyard and there were times when there was close to 150 people gathered there. There was always plenty of eating and drinking on these occasions. At one of these parties Rachel dressed up as 'Chico Marx'[20]. She always remembered this night because she ended up singing to all the guests. Rachel singing at the Purim party, dressed as a man, became an annual ritual. Despite no formal training she sang beautifully. She practiced by singing all day at home. Everyone knew whether Rachel was at home because of the singing.

Her mother could often be heard saying, "Shh! Rachelika esta cantando[21]." Their neighbour Alberto, who always played the accordion at the Seror family Purim parties, tried to persuade Rachel's father to take her to the studio so that she could sing on the radio. Israel Seror did not approve! "What?" he exclaimed, "No daughter of mine is going to be an entertainer."

---

[19] 'Clean Monday' is the Orthodox Christian equivalent to the Roman Catholic day 'Ash Wednesday' which is the first day of Lent.
[20] 'Chico Marx' is one of the three legendary 'Marx Brothers'. They were a Jewish-American comedy trio in the 1930s that had taken Hollywood by storm.
[21] *Spanish/Ladino* Rachel is singing.

"But she has such a beautiful voice," cried Alberto, "How can you allow that to go to waste?"

"I said no," replied her father, "And that's final."

On Purim night Alberto would begin the music by playing the accordion. He was joined by his brother who played the guitar and then Rachel would begin to sing. Usually, the first three songs were Ladino medleys which her grandmother had taught her. This was followed by her singing popular Greek songs.

After the songs, father would begin the dancing. He would place a Greek blues record on the gramophone and he would dance the zeibekiko[22]. No one understood this dance better than Rachel's father. It was a male dance that had no specific steps and Rachel's father performed it like it was part of his soul. He expressed each movement with intense emotions. After a while, the other men would join him on the dance floor. Towards the end of the evening, the blues which blared loudly from the phonograph's gold plated cylinder would be replaced with traditional Greek tunes. In the middle of the hacienda's courtyard there was a well which was encircled by the large party of guests holding hands and dancing the sirto[23] until long after midnight.

---

[22] A Greek folk dance with a rhythmic pattern of 9/8. It is considered an urban improvisational dance.

[23] A Greek open circle dance which is known as the oldest form of folk dancing.

Until the summer of 1940, the Seror family lived peacefully at the hacienda. Rachel was aware of a war that had broken out in the rest of Europe but it wasn't until Thursday the 13th of June 1940 when Rachel was returning home after having visited her aunt that she realized the imminent danger of the war. As she walked along Venizelou Avenue that afternoon, she saw many people running up to the newspaper vendor who was selling newspapers faster than he could handle. As Rachel got closer she heard the shouts of a young boy standing next to the newspaper seller yelling at the top of his lungs, "The Germans are 40 miles from Paris, the Germans are forty miles from Paris…"

She took 2 drachmas from her purse and lined up to buy herself a copy. She rushed home and showed the paper to everyone. Rachel sat quietly in the living room and read the front page story. A couple of hours later, when her father came from work, she immediately gave him the newspaper.

"I've already read it," he said, "Shimon came by and gave me a copy." Shimon was her father's youngest brother who was nineteen years old, the same age as her brother Moishe.

"Should we be worried?" she asked.

"Of course not," replied father, "The Germans have nothing to gain by invading Greece. The news today has caused a great stir because Paris is the city of all cities and everyone's finding it hard to believe that very soon it will be in German hands."

"My friend told me that the Germans are persecuting the Jews. Is that true?" asked Rachel.

"Yes it is, but as I already told you, we have nothing to worry about here." Rachel left the living room and went into the kitchen to help her mother prepare supper. She trusted her father and believed that he knew best.

She didn't concern herself with this subject again until two months later when her father's childhood friend came from America to visit them. According to Rachel's father, Samuel had always wanted to go to America since he was a young boy. His dream was realized when in the summer of 1917 Salonica tragically experienced a great fire that destroyed thousands of homes. Nearly half of Salonica's Jewish community was displaced including Samuel's family. Their home and his father's shoe repair shop were destroyed in the fire. He was nineteen years old at the time and took charge by contacting his mother's brother in America who sponsored the family. Eighteen months later, Samuel together with his parents', two sisters and one brother left for America. They settled in Baltimore, Maryland and within a few years Samuel opened his own shoe repair store. It was the only thing he knew how to do well since that's what his father, grandfather and great grandfather had done in Salonica for over a century. Over the years he corresponded with Rachel's father and had visited Salonica in 1932. Now he was coming for his second visit. It was August and Rachel's family had just returned from the Kassandra coast where they had spent the summer. Rachel's father insisted that Samuel stay at the hacienda for the duration of his trip which was four weeks.

The following Sunday, the family decided to take their visitor to Bexinari[24] where they spent the entire day. It was forty minutes away by tram and over the years it had slowly transformed into a mini amusement park by the sea with the most up to date swings, a number of restaurants and a huge playground where teenage boys played soccer and young girls played hopscotch.

When they arrived they visited Father's friend's cafeneion[25] where Rachel ordered loukoumades[26]- by far her favourite sweets. They all made their way down to the beach and swam in the lovely warm water. After her swim, Rachel sat on the sand to soak up the sun.

"Lola," yelled mother, "Come out of the water and lie down in the sun for a while."

Mother was a firm believer that if one sunbaked during the summer, you would not become ill during the winter. But it was nearly impossible to get Rachel's younger sister to come out of the water. She would have stayed in all day if she could have. Mother and grandma Joya laid out a tablecloth under one of the pine trees and they unloaded the picnic basket. This trip was made at least three times during the summer months when they weren't at their holiday home.

By six o'clock they had arrived back home. After dinner, as Rachel wandered outside into the courtyard she saw her father with his friend

---

[24] A small area in the district of Salonica.
[25] *Greek* Coffeehouse.
[26] Greek donuts that are traditionally served soaked in hot honey syrup, sprinkled with cinnamon and chopped walnuts.

Samuel sitting under the grapevines and reminiscing about their youth. This is when she heard Samuel pleading with her father, "Israel, you must sell everything and move away. It's going to be a very bad war."

"But it won't affect us here in Greece," said Rachel's father, "Besides how can I just pack up and leave our home? I really believe that Greece will be alright."

"I wouldn't be too sure about that! Can't you see what a megalomaniac Hitler is? He has already taken half of Europe."

Rachel's father's instincts were wrong this time, because only two months later, on the 28th of October, Greece was drawn into the Second World War when Mussolini's government gave Greece an ultimatum.

Greece was ordered to allow the Italian army to occupy the country and if they did not, they would be forcefully invaded. The Greek Prime Minister, Ioannis Metaxas, definitively responded on behalf of the Greek nation. He replied 'OXI'.[27]

On Friday 1st of November just before midday, the sound of war came to Salonica. Rachel was at her friend's house when a loud explosion resounded through the neighbourhood. Rachel and her friend Christina were in the living room and they fell to the ground, covering their heads with their hands as the bombing smashed all the windows. Broken glass flew everywhere. The bombing went on for at least twenty minutes and then everything was silent. After a while, Rachel and her friend tentatively stood up.

---

[27] *Greek* No

The following Sunday, the family decided to take their visitor to Bexinari[24] where they spent the entire day. It was forty minutes away by tram and over the years it had slowly transformed into a mini amusement park by the sea with the most up to date swings, a number of restaurants and a huge playground where teenage boys played soccer and young girls played hopscotch.

When they arrived they visited Father's friend's cafeneion[25] where Rachel ordered loukoumades[26]- by far her favourite sweets. They all made their way down to the beach and swam in the lovely warm water. After her swim, Rachel sat on the sand to soak up the sun.

"Lola," yelled mother, "Come out of the water and lie down in the sun for a while."

Mother was a firm believer that if one sunbaked during the summer, you would not become ill during the winter. But it was nearly impossible to get Rachel's younger sister to come out of the water. She would have stayed in all day if she could have. Mother and grandma Joya laid out a tablecloth under one of the pine trees and they unloaded the picnic basket. This trip was made at least three times during the summer months when they weren't at their holiday home.

By six o'clock they had arrived back home. After dinner, as Rachel wandered outside into the courtyard she saw her father with his friend

---

[24] A small area in the district of Salonica.
[25] *Greek* Coffeehouse.
[26] Greek donuts that are traditionally served soaked in hot honey syrup, sprinkled with cinnamon and chopped walnuts.

Samuel sitting under the grapevines and reminiscing about their youth. This is when she heard Samuel pleading with her father, "Israel, you must sell everything and move away. It's going to be a very bad war."

"But it won't affect us here in Greece," said Rachel's father, "Besides how can I just pack up and leave our home? I really believe that Greece will be alright."

"I wouldn't be too sure about that! Can't you see what a megalomaniac Hitler is? He has already taken half of Europe."

Rachel's father's instincts were wrong this time, because only two months later, on the 28th of October, Greece was drawn into the Second World War when Mussolini's government gave Greece an ultimatum.

Greece was ordered to allow the Italian army to occupy the country and if they did not, they would be forcefully invaded. The Greek Prime Minister, Ioannis Metaxas, definitively responded on behalf of the Greek nation. He replied 'OXI'.[27]

On Friday 1st of November just before midday, the sound of war came to Salonica. Rachel was at her friend's house when a loud explosion resounded through the neighbourhood. Rachel and her friend Christina were in the living room and they fell to the ground, covering their heads with their hands as the bombing smashed all the windows. Broken glass flew everywhere. The bombing went on for at least twenty minutes and then everything was silent. After a while, Rachel and her friend tentatively stood up.

---

[27] *Greek* No

"Are you alright?" asked Christina.

"Yes, I think so. How about you?"

"I'm alright," she replied.

They looked around in shock at all the broken window panes and were grateful to be unharmed.

"Let's go and see if the church was bombed," said Rachel.

"I'll do that," said Christina, "You go back to the hacienda to see if your family's alright. Then we'll meet at Elia's bakery at 2 o'clock. Hopefully we'll both have good news to share."

Both girls quickly ran out of the house. Christina ran towards the church where her father was the parish priest and Rachel ran all the way back to the hacienda. When she arrived home, she was relieved to see that her family was unharmed. Apart from a few bowls that lay in pieces on the kitchen floor, the hacienda had been untouched.

During the next week, Rachel noticed activity at the hacienda as her male relatives from other parts of Salonica came and went with shovels and other digging equipment. Her father, together with her two uncles who were also residing in the hacienda, had decided to build a bomb shelter where the courtyard was. This turned out to be a painstakingly slow process that lasted for one year. After three months, a temporary shelter was ready but only big enough for a family of four. When the big shelter was ready, the five families were able to live there. Rachel had the idea to turn the shelter into her own bedroom, but her parents wouldn't allow it.

The last two months of 1940 and the first two months of 1941 were exciting times for the Greek people as the newspapers were constantly reporting that the Greek army had pushed the Italians back into Albania. It was a time of great pride, as Italy's army was as large as the entire population of Greece. Rachel's family knew of three men who were fighting in Albania, one of whom was a relative. In late February, Rachel and her parents visited him at his home. He had fought at the Albanian front and was wounded in the leg before being discharged. He was unusually quiet, unlike his usual cheerful and talkative self. On their way home Rachel listened as her parents discussed how the savagery of war can change the characters of young men.

Soon it was March and it was that time of the year when Grandma Joya Capon's sewing room in the hacienda was filled with blue and white material. Rachel's maternal grandmother was undoubtedly one of the most well-known dressmakers in Salonica. She was constantly busy sewing, not only clothes for Rachel and all of her sisters but also wedding dresses and evening gowns. Most of her customers were non-Jews and by 1921 she had gained such a reputation that she was offered employment by the Salonica council to make hundreds of Greek flags annually, during the month of March. The 25th of March was Greek Independence Day when every school in Salonica would parade in front of politicians and distinguished guests in the city centre. Hundreds of flags of all different sizes were needed for this event. Grandma Joya was so busy that Rachel helped her whenever she could. She would cut up the material according to the pattern and she would place it on the table ready for her grandmother to sew. She made so many flags that when the hacienda received a spring clean every year, flags were found underneath sofas, squashed in between clothes and occasionally some had made their way onto the hacienda's grapevine.

This Independence Day was a very special one for Rachel. Since it was her last year in high-school this was going to be her last parade. Normally she wore a white top and a blue skirt as was required but a few select students wore the Greek National costumes. The female national costume was called the *amalia*[28] with its blue silk ankle-length skirt, its embroidered velvet vest and a cap with a long, golden tassel. This year for the first time Rachel was asked by one of her teachers if she would like to dress up in her country's national costume. She could hardly contain her excitement as she immediately said yes. She was then given an *amalia* costume to keep at home until the parade.

On the morning of the 25th of March 1941, the entire Seror family set out to the city centre. Rachel walked down the street with confidence and pride as passers-by told her how wonderful she looked.

As they got closer they were overwhelmed to see the huge crowds that had turned out. There had never been so many people. It was due not only to the fact that Greece was at war but also that it was winning.

---

[28] In the 19th century, Queen Amalia of Greece created a folksy court dress, which became a national Greek costume still known as the *Amalia dress*.

Once they arrived at the assembly point, Rachel went to line up with her school. For Rachel, the thrill of wearing the national costume was enormous and it got even better when one of the school's teachers gave her a large Greek flag to carry. She was then directed to the front of the line as she would be the one to lead her school during the parade. This moment was of such great significance for Rachel and her family. They celebrated it by taking plenty of photographs, not only at the parade but also at the hacienda when they returned. That evening they had a small get together of friends and family where they ate wonderful food and danced into the night.

After the meal, Rachel brought out a huge torte cake which she had ordered from the cake shop. This was a surprise for Christina's sister Evangelia who was celebrating her name day.

By ten o'clock in the evening the only guests still remaining were Rachel's friends, which included members of the Jewish youth groups of Zakynthos and Corfu[29]. They had two important things to celebrate. The first being their final year of high-school and the second being Greece's decisive victory over Italy. They began singing all of the patriotic songs that they had learnt at school. Rachel's second cousin walked in wearing his Greek military uniform with his arm in a sling. He had fought valiantly at the Albanian Front causing permanent damage to his right arm. Suddenly, the group erupted into a loud cheer and began singing the most popular song at the time. It was by Sophia Vebo and had been released

---

[29] Zakynthos and Corfu are two of the seven main islands in the Ionian sea.

during the winter of '40-'41. It was a send-up of Mussolini and the Italian army.

Duce[30] puts on his uniform
And his tall cap,
With all the feathers,
And one night with moon
He sets on to invade Greece,
The poor wretch.
On the mountains he meets with
Our brave evzones[31]
Who shock the master
The spaghetti eater…
…the Italians run like crazy towards the rocks
And from us and our Allies
They receive a kick,
And without many words
The Greek brave men have entered Korytsa[32].
"Oh! Ciano[33], I'll die, Ciano," cries Mussolini

---

[30] The Italian Fascist Party leader Benito Mussolini was identified by Fascists as *Il Duce* ("The Leader") of the movement.

[31] The Evzones are an historical elite light infantry and mountain units of the Greek Army.

[32] A town in south-eastern Albania whose inhabitants were Greek during antiquity.

[33] The Italian Foreign Minister from 1936-1943 and Benito Mussolini's son-in-law.

"Because in a while I'll lose Tirana³⁴ too."
The poor souls have suffered a great disaster,
And now Rome awaits its turn too.

The singing continued for a while and then Rachel decided to pay tribute to the Jewish youth who had come from Zakynthos and Corfu. She began singing one of her favourite *heptanesean*³⁵ *cantades*³⁶ to the sounds of the violin and mandolin. All her friends joined in the singing. Every time the word Zakynthos was sung the students from that island held up big banners with their island's name on it. The youth from Corfu did exactly the same.

If they could lower the mountains,
I'd be able to see Levante³⁷,
I'd be able to see Kephalonia,
And beautiful Zante³⁸.
Zakynthos and Kephalonia,
Corfu and Lefkada,

---

[34] Capital city of Albania.
[35] The seven islands in the Ionian Sea.
[36] Songs and/or serenades that are based on the popular Italian music of the early 19th century. It influenced the development of the Greek modern song to a considerable degree.
[37] In Italian, *Levante* means *The rising of the sun in the east.* In the 18th century during Venetian rule, Zakynthos was given the nickname *Il fiore di Levante-The flower of the east.*
[38] The Italian name for Zakynthos.

These four islands
Decorate Ellada[39].

They sang song after song and they did not stop until two o'clock in the morning. The great happiness and excitement that Rachel, her friends and family felt on that day was not to last long as the entire country was gripped with fear only twelve days later when the German army invaded Greece.

---

[39] The Greek word for Greece.

CHAPTER TWO

Challenging times in Salonica

On the morning of the sixth of April 1941, only twelve days after the eventful Independence Day party at the hacienda, Rachel's family received news that would be life-changing for them. It was a Sunday, the day of rest for the majority of Greeks. For the Jewish community, their day of rest was a Saturday and therefore Rachel's father had gone to his workshop as usual. He returned home early that day. Instead of coming home at two o'clock, he walked in at eleven that morning, looking disturbed.

"You're home early," said mother, with Rachel standing behind her holding the feather duster in her hand. As school was closed on Sundays mother always had some household chores for Rachel to do.

"I have some bad news," he said.

Rachel and mother stared at him with anxious anticipation.

"Raoul came by the shop and told me that the Germans have invaded Yugoslavia and any minute now they will invade Greece if they haven't already."

"Are you sure?" asked mother.

"Yes," he replied with hopelessness all over his face.

This was very serious news. The border with Yugoslavia was only fifty miles away from Salonica. Everyone realised that the Germans could enter Salonica by nightfall. Rachel's father immediately told his family to pack a light travel bag. He was determined to take his family away from Salonica. He did not want to be there when the Germans invaded as he was certain there would be bombing and chaos. The entire family was ready in an hour. They all walked down to the port where they hired a small boat and skipper. They made their way down the Thermaic Gulf. It was a boat ride that Rachel and her family had taken many times but never under such circumstances. For the first time ever, Rachel was frightened of the unknown and the uncertainty that awaited them. Half an hour later, they arrived at Angelochori. They disembarked and made their way to their father's cousin's boarding house. He was waiting for them. A decade earlier, this large building had been turned into a pensione.[40] Rachel and her family moved into two of the rooms. There they listened to the wireless and heard the news of Germany's invasion of Greece. The news described how the German army was moving down towards Salonica. As a consequence, the following two days saw the arrival of more family members who were trying to stay ahead of the invading enemy. On the 9th of April it was announced on the radio that Salonica had been invaded without much resistance. There were no bombings and no fighting in the streets. Many of the residents had escaped to the countryside, leaving the usually vibrant city looking more like a ghost town.

In Angelochori, Rachel's family together with their extended family waited patiently for incoming news and updates. Ten days after their arrival some of their relatives began leaving to go back to Salonica.

---

[40] *Italian* A small hotel or boarding house.

Rachel's father decided to wait another week. They were the last to leave the pensione.

On the 23rd of April the family boarded a boat and took the half hour ride up the Thermaic gulf to Salonica. As they approached the port, they could see that the Greek flag which usually flew above the city's historic 'White Tower'[41], had now been replaced with the Nazi flag. That's when it hit Rachel that her country was being occupied by a foreign power. On the short walk back home from the port, they saw the first enemy soldiers. If not for their uniforms, they could have been tourists, walking about, smoking, talking with one another and laughing.

Back at the hacienda, some other family members had already returned from Larissa and Ioannina where they had moved to for their safety. Four days later on the 27th of April the Germans invaded Athens. They were in shock as it was now official - Greece had fallen to the enemy.

Despite the presence of an occupying force, the next few months were quite uneventful except for the changes that everyone had to keep up with. The rich diversity of produce that was sold at the downtown market was becoming sparser by the day. The three families of the hacienda decided to grow their own vegetables. The courtyard already had a lemon tree, a fig tree, a plum tree, an apricot tree and a grapevine. Behind the hacienda was a plot of land where the families got to work and began digging and

---

[41] The 'White Tower' is a monument and museum on the waterfront of the city of Salonica. It was built by the Ottoman Turks in the 15th century to fortify the city's harbour.

planting. They grew tomatoes, cucumbers, zucchinis and red peppers. By July the three families were able to rely on these home grown vegetables for their fresh produce.

Rachel was dealing with her own changes as she had finished her education and was fortunate to have found a part-time job at a printer. She was taught how to use the machinery but was not paid during her training. When her training was complete she was given a box of *Turkish delights*[42] and an offer of part-time work. She earned 25 drachmas a week which wasn't a lot but she didn't have a family to feed and she lived with her parents. She spent the money on herself buying lipsticks, perfume and shoes. Unfortunately, this was not to last. In October 1941 the owner of the printing works told Rachel that he could no longer pay her. This happened regularly during the German occupation which imposed severe economic hardship on Greece. Rachel's boss said she could continue to work as a volunteer but after discussing it with her parents, Rachel decided to leave and stayed at home with her mother and helped her to run the household.

One of her first duties was to take a glass of olive oil to the Synagogue once a week. She would empty the glass into a shiny brass cauldron which hung from the ceiling. The oil, which was delivered to the Synagogue by each Jewish family, was used to keep the sanctuary lamp eternally lit as was required according to the book of Exodus 27: 20-21.

---

[42] A fragrant sweet cube of jelly that is heavily dusted with icing sugar.

The *eternal flame* hung in front of the ark as a symbol of God's eternal presence.

One afternoon, Rachel set out with the glass of olive oil wrapped in a kitchen towel to deliver it to the Synagogue. When she arrived, she noticed a huge black car parked in front of the Synagogue. There was a German soldier standing and smoking next to the car. She quickly made her way up the steps and into the Synagogue. As she entered the foyer she saw two men dressed in suits wearing fedora hats who were talking to the Rabbi. She scurried past them and as she was about to enter the Synagogue hall, a voice echoed,

"Mademoiselle[43]?"

Rachel stopped and turned around. One of the men motioned for her to approach him. She slowly walked towards them. One of the men took out a baton and struck the package that Rachel was carrying. The blow was so forceful that not only did the glass of olive oil fall and shatter into pieces but Rachel fell down as well. Both of the men stared contemptuously at the mess and turned and walked out. The Rabbi helped Rachel up and two women ran out from the office to offer assistance.

"I'm terribly sorry," said the Rabbi.

"It wasn't your fault," said Rachel, "But who were they?"

"The Gestapo[44]," replied the Rabbi, "They've heard rumours that we are helping the resistance."

"Are we?" asked Rachel.

---

[43] *French* Miss.
[44] The official secret police of Nazi Germany and German-occupied Europe.

The Rabbi did not reply instead he excused himself and went into his office. The two office workers gave Rachel a glass of water as she sat trying to compose herself. She returned home and once she was inside the hacienda her emotions got the better of her and she began to cry.
"What happened?" asked father.
Rachel explained what had happened and then made it clear that she wouldn't be delivering the glass of olive oil ever again. Her father and brother took over that job from then onwards.

The winter of 1941-942 was uneventful as Rachel found herself staying at home more and spending time with her grandmother either playing cards or helping her with her sewing. Food became increasingly difficult to buy that winter. The five families at the hacienda came to rely heavily on the food they grew in their garden. Even Grandma Joya was seen tending the citrus trees that she had planted herself. However, whether it was because of lack of food, or stressful living conditions, Grandma Joya's health began to deteriorate. She was in constant pain and could not go anywhere without her walking stick. Her ongoing rheumatism had flared up worse than ever before. Their local pharmacy had run out of soothing cream specially made for such ailments and their family doctor did not have any more medication for pain relief. The doctor suggested that once spring set in, Grandma should go to Volos for a mud bath.
"We're living in precarious times," he said, "But if you are able to, it's worth making the trip."

For around fifteen years, Rachel's grandmother had made the annual trip to Volos, 215 km south of Salonica. Volos is on the east coast of the mainland of Greece. The mineral rich springs are in a small village in the hills. The spa was used for therapeutic purposes. Visitors immersed themselves in three tubs. The first one was filled with mud and it was customary to soak in the mud tub for ninety minutes. Then you entered the second tub which contained the mineral rich spring water. Here you removed the mud with a sponge. The third tub was also filled with spring water. One soaked in it for fifteen minutes as therapy and to remove any excess mud.

Rachel's mother insisted that Grandma Joya go to Volos. Initially, she refused to go because of the expense. The hardship of war was tough on the family. They were living from day to day not knowing how long their food supplies would last. Grandma thought that the mud bath was an unnecessary luxury. Eventually she agreed to going but only if Rachel went with her since they shared a special bond. In early June, Rachel and her grandmother set off for Volos where they would stay for two weeks. On the day of their departure, a taxi took them to the main railway station in Salonica. There they boarded a train and nearly four hours later they arrived in Volos. After a twenty minute taxi ride, they arrived at their hotel and spa retreat deep inside the forest. Rachel loved the surrounding area as it reminded her of a fairy tale setting. The trees were very green and the flowers were in full bloom. She and her grandmother would go on many walks in the dense forest and when grandma Joya was having her mud bath, which was three times a week, Rachel would wander around by herself in the rich landscape.

On one of these days when Rachel was alone, taking a long walk around the retreat, she saw a woman walking towards her holding the hands of two toddlers. She smiled at her and Rachel smiled back. She then stopped and spoke to Rachel. It was difficult for Rachel to understand what the woman was saying until she realised that the woman was deaf. Rachel took delight in getting to know this lovely lady and her two beautiful children. Her name was Stella and they quickly became friends. Stella was also from Salonica and Jewish as well. Rachel introduced Grandma Joya to her new friend, only to discover that Grandma had met her ten years before, when Stella was sixteen years old.

When it was time for Rachel and Grandma to go back home, they exchanged addresses and Stella gave Rachel her telephone number. On the day of their departure, Stella and her children accompanied Rachel and Grandma Joya to the Volos railway station and stood there waving as the train left the station. An hour into their journey, a large group of German soldiers got onto the train at one of the stops. The train was already full, so some of the soldiers ended up standing right next to Rachel and Grandma's seats. Rachel pretended to ignore them by staring out of the window the entire time. Much to Rachel's discomfort, the soldiers stayed standing there until the train reached Salonica where Rachel and her grandmother got off.

A few weeks later, Rachel decided to contact Stella. She had been unable to forget her as she felt they were kindred spirits. Stella insisted that she come over immediately. Rachel already had her address and she knew that the location of her home was right on the port in one of the apartment buildings. When she arrived she pressed the buzzer and Stella's voice was heard through the intercom, "Come up," she said. Rachel took the elevator to the top floor and as she exited the elevator she realised that there was only one apartment door. She rang the doorbell and in a few seconds Stella opened the door with a huge smile on her face. Rachel entered the apartment and was awe-struck by its size and the exquisite, modern style in which it was decorated. She had never seen anything like it before.

"I've only seen these types of homes in the movies," said Rachel, "Your home is absolutely beautiful."

Stella explained to Rachel that it belonged to her father-in-law who was an Italian Baron. Whenever they were in Salonica this is where they stayed. She then spoke of how, as a student at the deaf school in Rome, she had been introduced to her husband by her own father who had gone to Italy for business. Her father and husband did business together and one evening Stella went out to dinner with them.

"He just really liked me," she said shyly.

Rachel was not surprised because of Stella's great beauty. Rachel thought she looked like the legendary Helen of Troy.

Rachel was somewhat surprised that Stella's husband was not Jewish.

"My father did not care that Enzo was not Jewish. He was grateful that there was a man of means who wanted to marry me," said Stella.

Rachel surmised that Stella's father did not believe a handicapped woman had the privilege of being fussy.

"Is your husband here in Salonica?" asked Rachel.

"Yes," she replied, "We will be staying in Salonica for the next few years, that I am sure of."

After spending a few hours with her new found friend, Rachel politely excused herself and extended an invitation to Stella and her family to come to the hacienda.

"I'm not sure if my husband can come but the children and I would love to come to your home."

It was to be that Stella never did come to the hacienda. The next time Rachel saw her again was under the most extraordinary circumstances, as horrifying events had impacted their lives.

CHAPTER THREE

Forty-five Desperate Days

By February 1943 the Jews of Salonica, along with their fellow Greeks, were trying to survive day by day as food rationing became worse. There had been no mass actions against the Jews in Salonica since July 1942 when nine thousand Jewish males had been ordered to appear at Liberty Square where they were humiliated and beaten by the German soldiers. This lull was not to last.

Rachel and her brother Moishe were shocked into the reality of the occupation one morning when they were at the Maccabi[45] club. The club was a large complex in Salonica that had opened in 1908. It was equipped with every imaginable sporting facility and was used by the entire Jewish community.

During the summer months Rachel and her sister Lola would often go and play tennis there. Rachel never forgot being scolded by their mother for having clay all over their tennis clothes.

"We need to change our clay court surface to grass," said Rachel many times, "Just like the one in Corfu."

---

[45] The word Maccabi is the name given to Jewish sports clubs around the world. It comes from the name *Maccabees*, a family of Jewish patriots who fought for and liberated Judea from Syrian rule in 142 BC.

The tennis courts of Corfu had been established by the British in the nineteenth century therefore consisted of a grass surface.

"Until that happens, I can only dream about it," replied mother as she struggled to remove the clay from the white clothes, using a lot of bleach. During the winter months, the sisters would spend long rainy days at the club playing table tennis. However, there was another reason why Rachel and her sister Lola enjoyed going to the Maccabi club all year round and that was to mingle with the well-known sports stars. Having seen their pictures in the newspaper, the sisters were able to recognize them. This was very exciting as these sports stars represented Greece in the Maccabi Games, the Balkan Games and of course the Olympic Games.

Rachel's older brother Moishe was a keen ice-skater and since there was a permanent ice-skating rink at the club, he skated all year round. Rachel and Lola skated with him many times and they were in awe of their brother as he skated with such flair.

In 1933, when Moishe was twelve years old, he caught the eye of an ice-skating coach. He took him under his wing and prepared him to compete at an international level. He was to try out for the 1940 Olympic winter games. The qualifying competition was to take place in September of 1939. Moishe's family hardly saw him before the competition as he practised every day for three months.

"If I had known it was going to be like this, I would have transported his bed over to the Maccabi club," joked father, "I've lost my son! I don't see him anymore."

"You know how important this is to him," replied mother.

"Trust me, I know only too well."

Moishe would never get the chance to try out for the Greek Olympic winter team as the war in Europe broke out in early September of 1939. Needless to say, all winter sporting trials were put on hold.

During this time Rachel overheard Moishe's coach tell him something that would haunt her forever.

"With a bit of luck the war will be over by 1943 and you can try to qualify for the team then."

The sad reality was that the entire Seror family, with the exception of Rachel, would be transported to Auschwitz[46] in 1943.

One morning in mid-February 1943, Rachel and her brother Moishe had gone to the Maccabi Club early as Moishe had a practice session with his coach. Rachel decided not to do any sports that day. Instead she was a spectator at the ice skating venue. She sat back and watched her brother do the same manoeuvre over and over again until his coach was satisfied. There were other skaters there, either practising or skating purely for enjoyment. As Rachel sat back admiring her brother's skating ability, there was a sudden announcement on the loud speaker saying that everyone has to leave the building immediately. She saw two men standing next to the skating rink. They were dressed just like the two men that she had encountered at the synagogue eighteen months earlier. She realised that they were the Gestapo. She calmly got up and went to the edge of the rink and waited for her brother. As they left the club, they saw

---

[46] A Nazi death camp situated in the south-west part of Poland during World War II.

German soldiers holding machine guns. The soldiers had surrounded the building. Rachel and Moishe returned home hardly saying a word to each other.

When they arrived home, they saw their mother and grandmother walking around anxiously. They were looking for yellow material in the three trunks where they kept the girls' trousseaus.

"Here it is," said Grandma Joya, picking up a folded piece of yellow cloth, "This should be enough for all of us."

Rachel and Moishe stood there staring at her.

"Enough for what?" asked Moishe.

Before anyone could reply, father came inside the hacienda.

"The Germans have introduced new laws for the Jews, which we have to abide by," he said.

"But what's the yellow material for?" asked Rachel.

"We all have to wear a yellow star on the left hand side of our chest, next to the heart."

"What kind of a star?" she asked.

"One that represents the *Star of David*[47]," replied father.

"Are you serious?"

"Do I look like I'm joking?" yelled father with his hands raised up in the air.

Rachel and Moishe looked at each other before walking away quietly. Their uncle from the house at the back of the hacienda came into their

---

[47] A six-pointed figure consisting of two interlaced equilateral triangles, used as a Jewish and Israeli symbol. It represents either the shape of King David's shield or the emblem on it during biblical times.

home with the newspaper and showed them all the restrictions that had been placed upon the Jews.

The Jews were no longer permitted to work as lawyers, physicians and professors. They were barred from public transportation and were forbidden from belonging to any club or institution.

Rachel's family was in complete shock with these new laws as was the entire Jewish community of Salonica. As law abiding citizens they went ahead and adhered to every restriction placed upon them. Two days later, Rachel and her entire family went to the town hall as all the Jews of Salonica had been ordered to do. There were hundreds of people waiting in line. It was rumoured that they would each receive a new paper identity document with a number on it. Each person had to write their number with black ink on their yellow star, which Rachel and her family duly did.

In the next few days, people all over Salonica began appearing out in public with a yellow star on their left upper lapel. This had created uneasiness amongst the gentile population. Two weeks after they had been ordered to wear the star, Rachel's friend Christina told her how a public protest was going to take place in the main town square demanding that the Jews of Salonica should not wear a yellow star. Two days later, the protest was aborted. The protest leaders had received information that the Germans would not hesitate to take drastic retaliatory measures if such a demonstration was to go ahead. For the next few weeks Rachel's family along with all the Jewish citizens of Salonica were forced to endure the humiliation of being branded every time they left their homes. Rachel however, was determined to rebel against these laws. Every time she left the hacienda, she made sure to wear a jacket so as to keep the yellow star hidden. It was her way of resisting the enemy.

As the days passed, the situation went from bad to worse. New orders were issued. This time they were far more severe. All the Jews of Salonica were ordered to leave their homes and move into another area of the city. They were given forty-eight hours to organise everything. The Baron Hirsch district, which was two and a half miles away from the hacienda, was to be turned into a ghetto for the Jews. All the gentiles living there were also given forty-eight hours to evacuate and they were moved to another area. It just so happened that uncle Baruch, Rachel's father's brother, lived in the Baron Hirsch district. He was an engineer by trade and he was employed by the railways. His house was walking distance from the Baron Hirsch railway station, which for the next five months would end up becoming the departure point for nearly all of Salonica's Jews.

Rachel's father was advised by many people to go into hiding. He decided that he and his family would not hide because they were law abiding citizens who had nothing to hide.

"We will go and stay with my brother," he said, "I'm sure it will all turn out alright if we do as we're told."

They had also been instructed to take only what they could carry. Rachel packed and unpacked her small travel bag several times. She had no clue what to include, so in the end she put in two of her favourite dresses, one jacket, a skirt, her black shoes, a pair of white bobby socks, her lipsticks and perfume. She placed her family's photographs in her hand bag. On the morning of the evacuation, the five families of the hacienda gathered at the front entrance. Despite there being twenty-five people standing there, it was awfully quiet. Rachel recalls the sad look on everyone's faces. At nine o'clock, the Greek police came to escort them to the ghetto. As they walked, Rachel noticed that two German soldiers were following the group. She also noticed that one of the two policemen wore a black armband with a yellow star on it. She was to learn later on that the Jewish policemen of the Salonican police force were ordered to wear these armbands. They were designated to keep law and order in the ghetto and as payment they received a loaf of bread every second day. As the Seror family walked silently towards their new location, Rachel felt that the situation was surreal and it was difficult to comprehend what was actually going on.

Once they had arrived at the Baron Hirsch railway station terminal, they were told to stop. As Rachel gazed ahead she could see barbed wire fencing going right around the block. She looked up she saw a watch tower with a German soldier in it, holding a machine gun. Rachel would soon discover that the ghetto had three watch towers, one at every entrance. She felt sick to her stomach as she realised the terrible reality of the situation. A whistle sound pierced the air and the crowd began to move again. They walked through a gate and Rachel's father led his family to her Uncle Baruch's house.

Despite having a big house, the spacious rooms became very cramped. Within two weeks, fifty-five family members were living in the house. Each family shared one room. At times, the cramped conditions became unbearable, but it was still better than living in any of the other run down apartments.

In the ghetto, no one was permitted to go to work and most people wandered around all day. Rachel decided that in order to have something to do, she would volunteer at the hospital. It was the biggest hospital in Salonica at the time and it fell within the jurisdiction of the ghetto. It was a Jewish hospital but had cared for all citizens until February 1943 when the anti-Jewish laws came into effect. Rachel helped to wash patients and whatever else she was asked to do. It was much better than hanging around her uncle's over-cramped house. An added bonus was that she was able to bring to her family a loaf of bread which she took from the hospital kitchen at the end of her shift.

All of the food stores in the ghetto had closed down. Food had become so scarce that many people had begun begging on street corners. One day as Rachel was walking home, she saw the Greeks outside of the ghetto throwing loaves of bread and tinned food over the barbed wire fence into the ghetto. People scrambled to pick up whatever they could as they were clearly starving.

In the meantime, the German soldiers yelled, "Geht weg", as they pointed their guns to the Greek Christians who were throwing the food into the ghetto.[48]

---

[48] *German* Go away

Rachel remembers coming back from the hospital one afternoon to the smell of cooked meat. Things became so desperate that her uncle Baruch had killed his horse and was cooking the meat. Rachel refused to have any as she felt sick at the thought of eating horse meat.

After one week in the ghetto Rachel was to witness for the first time in her life something unforgettably awful. One morning, as she walked towards the hospital, she saw two German soldiers shoot a man with their machine guns. She had never seen anything so violent before. She hurried along as fast as she could and when she arrived at the hospital, she locked herself in the room where all the linen was kept. She crouched down and then began to sob. She did not work on her shift that day as she spent ages sitting on the floor. After a few hours she managed to get up and decided to go back home. When she arrived home, her brother told her that a man was gunned down earlier on.

"I was there," she said, "Why was he killed?"

"He hadn't handed over all his money, so that's why he was shot," said Moishe.

"And how did the Germans find out that he still had some money on him?"

"I think he was chosen randomly to be frisked."

Rachel became terrified as she had 45 drachmas in her bag. That evening she was not able to sleep as she tossed and turned not knowing what to do about the money. The following morning she gave the money to her mother before leaving for the hospital.

After twelve long days in the ghetto, Rachel heard from her brother Moishe that her friend Christina wanted to see her. Moishe had friends who smuggled themselves in and out of the ghetto and they had been approached by Christina. The next day, at three o'clock in the afternoon, Rachel met up with Christina at the barbed wire fence.

"Don't worry," said Christina, "I'll find a way to get you out of here."

Rachel stood there staring at her.

"Meet me again in two days, at three o'clock at this spot. I will then tell you what needs to be done," said Christina.

She turned and walked away. Rachel remained standing there until Christina had disappeared around the corner.

That evening, Rachel told her father that her friend had a plan to take her out of the ghetto.

"You're not going anywhere alone," said father, "You'll come with us, wherever that may be."

By this stage the deportations of the Salonican Jews had already begun. Every third day there was a list of family names posted on an outside wall. All of those whose names were on the list, had to leave the next morning. No one knew where they were being taken. Everyone assumed that they were being transported to somewhere in Germany to work.

Two days later, Rachel went to the barbed wire fence as Christina had instructed. Her friend was already there waiting for her.

"I can't come with you," said Rachel, "My father won't let me. I have to go with my family."

"It's better for you to come and stay with us," said Christina, "Why go to Germany where you'll probably have to work day and night. If we had more room, I would gladly take in your family but we only have room for one person."

"I don't know what to do," said Rachel.

"Come and stay with us. When the war is over you will see your family again. Here, take this envelope," she said before bending down and pushing it under the barbed wire fence.

Rachel quickly picked it up and put it in her handbag.

"I'll see you again in two days," said Christina, "But before I leave there's one more thing that I have to give you. Take this and quickly leave before a German soldier comes."

She then took a step back and threw a small parcel over the fence. Rachel quickly picked it up and went home. Once inside the room that she and her family were living in, she saw that the parcel contained a loaf of bread, some olives and feta cheese which she shared with her family. In the envelope there was a letter stating that until she leaves the ghetto she must meet Christina every second day at three o'clock at the usual spot.

Twenty-two days after moving into the ghetto, Rachel's father's name was posted on the wall. Upon hearing the news, Rachel went down to the location where the names were posted to see for herself. As her eyes scanned down the columns of names, she came across her father's name.

Names:	Departure point:	Date:
Time:		
Israel Moishe Seror	Salonica Railway	Tuesday
9 AM	Station	30 March 1943

Rachel felt a shiver go up her spine as she stared at his name. The departure date was the following day. She didn't have much time to decide what to do. Should she go with her family or go into hiding at her friend's house? As she walked back to Uncle Baruch's house she thought of everything that Christina had told her. Why go to some unknown location in Germany and be forced to work from morning to night. After all, there were rumours that had already begun to circulate that the Germans were losing the war. She was certain that it was all going to be over very soon. She then made her final decision. She was going to go into hiding.

When she arrived home, Rachel saw her mother packing a small bag. She was told to go and pack her bag for herself. She knew then that she had to come up with a story as to why she wouldn't be leaving with them. The truth was out of the question. Her father would never agree to Rachel leaving the ghetto to go and stay with people who were not family. She searched for her father and found him at the back of the house where he was talking with her uncles.

"Baba," said Rachel, "I'm not going with you tomorrow. I'm going to stay with Uncle Baruch."

"Why?" asked father.

"Because it's better if I come with my aunt and uncle on the next transport."
Rachel's father didn't seem to like the idea and before he had time to speak, Uncle Baruch interrupted, "Don't worry Israel, I'm sure that my name will be on the list soon, so when we leave I'll take Rachel with us."
"Alright," said father hesitantly, "Stay with your uncle and make sure to come with him."

The next morning Rachel got up early and helped her mother pack. She then dressed her two little sisters and gave them some warm milk to drink. Rachel's mother asked her to take Lola's temperature as she suspected that Lola had a fever because she was red in the face and sweating. Lola did have a temperature, so mother took out her red lipstick and smudged some colour on Lola's lips. She didn't want to take any chances because everyone was aware of the fact that the Nazis were known to shoot people in the ghetto just because they were ill. Rachel gave mother her woollen scarf and she wrapped it around Lola's head to keep her warm.
The entire family gathered at the front door, and those leaving kissed everyone who was staying behind.
"I'll see you in a few days, God willing," said Uncle Baruch as he hugged his brother.
Rachel kissed her mother, her father, her brother, her grandmother and her three sisters. They walked away and she stood at the door looking at them until they were out of sight.

Rachel went back inside the house and sat there all alone in the room that she had shared with her family for three weeks. She had already begun to miss them and contemplated the idea of leaving with her uncle Baruch when it was his time to go. She lay down on one of the beds and dozed off only to be woken by Uncle Baruch's wife, Aunt Rachel. Because they shared the same name, they seemed to have a special bond.

"Come to the kitchen," said Aunt Rachel, "I'll make us Turkish coffee." For the next two days Rachel waited patiently to meet her friend. In the meantime, she played with her two little cousins, and they reminded her of her own sisters. Her aunt Rachel had experienced difficulty in conceiving but after meeting with a Moroccan Rabbi, who often visited Salonica and was known to create miracles for barren women, she became pregnant. She ended up having two beautiful daughters very close together.

On the third day after her family had left, Rachel discovered that Uncle Baruch's name had been posted on the list. She knew that they were leaving the following morning and by all accounts she was supposed to go with them. That entire morning Rachel was concocting reasons to tell them why she couldn't go with them. She was in such a precarious situation because she did not know when her friend would be ready to take her out of the ghetto. That afternoon, Rachel made her way to the spot at the barbed wire fence where Christina was waiting for her. She approached her with caution as there were a few German soldiers around, talking and smoking.

"We've got everything organised," said Christina, "It's tonight at six o'clock sharp. Make sure to be here and don't bring a bag with you."

"My uncle and aunt are being transported out tomorrow," said Rachel.

"Then it's perfect timing," said Christina as she quickly turned and left before anyone spotted her.

On her way back Rachel had butterflies in her stomach, she knew that in a few hours she would be making her escape. She hurried to her room and searched through her clothes to see if she could take anything that she could carry. Her eyes settled on her father's tallit.[49] She picked it up and put it against her face and began to sob. She was determined to take it with her so she decided to use it as a scarf since she had given hers to her sister a few days earlier. She realised that there wasn't anything else that she could take with her. Rachel managed to fit a few small family photographs in her pocket. At a quarter to six that evening she left her room.

"Where are you going?" asked Uncle Baruch as he passed her in the passage.

"My friend's coming to give me a food parcel," replied Rachel, "I won't be long."

"Curfew time began nearly an hour ago," he said, "Don't risk it! We're leaving tomorrow."

"That's why I have to go. I need the parcel for our journey."

"Alright," said Uncle Baruch, "But be very careful and hurry back."

---

[49] The Hebrew word *tallit* refers to a rectangular *prayer shawl* that is traditionally worn during morning prayers on weekdays and during Jewish holidays. All tallit have four knotted fringes that are attached at each corner.

"I will," said Rachel as she walked out into the cool crisp wind.

Since being in the ghetto, she had never gone out after sunset. The streets were completely deserted and the street lights were turned off. She began hurrying along until she turned the corner, then she stopped for a moment as she had come to an open area where the searchlights from the watch tower lit up the entire street. She suddenly felt terrified, knowing that if she was spotted she would be shot. She stood there for while as the searchlight continued to light up the street every twenty seconds. After the fourth time she decided to make a run for it, but in her haste she fell right in the middle of the street. She got to her feet and continued to run, just missing the searchlight. At the next turn she saw the lights were on in the corner house and a woman standing just outside her front door.

"Where are you off to?" she asked Rachel.

"My friend has brought me a food parcel. I'm going to pick it up."

"I'm waiting for my husband," said the woman, "He went outside the ghetto this morning and he still hasn't come back."

"Do you know which transport you're on?" asked Rachel.

"No," said the woman, "Our name has not been on the list yet."

"I have to run," said Rachel, realising that it was probably past six o'clock.

"Be careful," said the stranger, as Rachel ran off along the sidewalk.

As she approached the final street she noticed two German soldiers standing and making idle chatter. Rachel's heart began to beat so fast that she felt herself becoming hot despite the cold chill in the air.

"That's it Rachel," she anxiously whispered under her breath, "I have two choices before me - death or freedom. Whatever happens, it's meant to be."

She then stopped shaking and decided to take the long way round.

At last she approached the spot where she was told to be and she saw her friend Christina with her sister Evangelia waiting for her. The two sisters had already cut the barbed wire at the bottom and she could see Evangelia holding up the wires.

"Hurry," said Christina, as Rachel bent down and started to crawl under the fence. Suddenly there was some kind of whistling sound that made the three girls stop dead in their tracks. They were terrified because although they weren't in the path of the searchlight, they were directly below the watch tower.

Rachel continued to crawl as Christina pulled her along. Rachel's stocking got stuck on the wire but she pulled herself free. As she stood up she saw the police station on the corner, with the Greek policeman standing there pretending not to notice anything. Rachel found out later that Christina's father was the policeman's family's parish priest and he had been told of the escape plan.

Christina quickly placed a shawl over Rachel and made sure that it covered the yellow star. The two sisters held onto Rachel's arms as they walked briskly through the streets of Salonica. As they walked, Rachel felt something running down the side of her right leg. It was blood. The wire had not only ripped her stocking but it had pierced her skin too. Through the panic of it all Rachel hadn't felt anything until that moment. She did not care about the pain because at last she was out of the ghetto. Rachel was finally free.

CHAPTER FOUR

In Hiding

It was approaching seven o'clock as Rachel and her two friends hurried as fast as they could along the streets of Salonica.

"In two minutes curfew begins," said Evangelia as she looked at her watch for the umpteenth time.

"Just continue walking," said Christina, "We're nearly there."

Since the arrival of the Germans, a curfew time had been imposed on the city of Salonica. During the spring and summer months, the curfew began at eight o'clock in the evening and ended at six o'clock in the morning. During the autumn and winter, the curfew time was from seven o'clock in the evening until seven o'clock in the morning. The curfew time in the ghetto however, differed. For the short few months of the ghettos existence, the hours of curfew were from six o'clock in the evening until eight o'clock in the morning. Anyone caught outside on the street during this time would be shot on sight, no questions asked. The girls continued to walk, speeding up their pace, until they came to a junction where they suddenly stopped. A *cafeneio*[50] on the opposite side of the road was filled with German soldiers. There were even some soldiers sitting and drinking

---

[50] *Greek* Coffeehouse.

outside in front of the *cafeneio*. There were bottles of *ouzo*[51] and caskets of *retsina*[52] on the tables.

"What are we going to do now?" asked Evangelia.

"We'll have to wait," replied Christina.

"But it's already ten minutes past curfew time."

"So what do you suggest we do?" asked Christina.

"Let's turn back and go down Aphrodite Avenue," said Rachel.

Both sisters looked at her, "I think that will work," said Christina.

"Trust me it will," said Rachel, "I grew up in this area. I know it like the back of my hand."

Aphrodite Avenue was where the hacienda was located. The three girls stared at every house and hacienda they passed. They were all eerily silent. When they came to the Seror family home, Rachel pulled away from the girls and stood in front of the double doors. She pushed the lion's head handle but the door did not open. Rachel went to the right of the hacienda to her parents' bedroom window but she could not see in through the closed shutters. She then stood there waiting desperately to hear her mother scolding her for being late. She would have given anything just to hear her dear mother's voice again. Christina put her hand on Rachel's shoulder. "Come on," she said gently, "We haven't got long to go."

The three girls continued to walk arm in arm. Ten minutes later, they arrived at Christina and Evangelia's home. They opened the front entrance door and walked quietly upstairs to their apartment.

---

[51] Ouzo is an anise-flavoured spirit that is widely consumed in Greece and Cyprus.
[52] Greek wine flavoured with resin.

"Where have you been?" asked Father Nikolas.

"Sorry baba," said Christina, "We had to take a detour because the Germans were having a party at Manoli's cafeneio."

Then both Father Nikolas and his wife greeted Rachel. She couldn't thank them enough. She was so grateful for their kindness. They took Rachel to the bathroom and got her to sit on a stool. Christina's mother walked in holding disinfectant lotion and gauze. In no time they had treated Rachel's leg wound and bandaged it up.

They then took Rachel to her new bedroom. She was given Evangelia's room who had moved in with her sister.

"This isn't right," said Rachel, "Let me move in with Christina and Evangelia can have her bedroom back."

But both sisters with their mother insisted on Rachel having her own room.

Rachel could not believe the family's generosity, especially at a time when acts of betrayal were generously rewarded by the enemy.

After settling herself in to her new room, Rachel went to the dining room where they all sat and had dinner. The warmth and atmosphere of that evening brought tears to Rachel's eyes as she thought of her own family who she had last seen just a few days ago. After the meal Rachel got up to help with the dishes but they all insisted that since she would be living with them for a while, she was exempt from washing up on the first night. Instead, she sat in the sitting room with Father Nikolas as he told her his life story.

He was a Russian Orthodox priest who had come from Sevastopol, Russia. As a twenty year old, he had escaped with his life from the Seminary where he was studying. It was 1918 and Russia was in the midst of a revolution. These were indeed troubled times as only a year earlier the Tzar[53] and his entire family had been murdered as Russia fell into the hands of the Communists. At the time, Father Nikolas was a deacon who, together with two more deacons and a Bishop, arrived in Sofia, Bulgaria. They stayed there for three months before Father Nikolas was sent to a Seminary school in Salonica to finish his studies.

Before he was ordained he had married a local Greek woman who herself was the daughter of a priest. They had two daughters, the oldest one being Rachel's best friend, Christina.

That night Rachel slept soundly for the first time in a long time. The anxiety of living precariously day by day in the ghetto had finally lifted. The next morning she found herself alone in the house. She had slept in and so went into the bathroom, brushed her teeth and washed her face. She got dressed and went back into her bedroom and sat there until Christina returned with her mother. They had gone out to a nearby wilderness on the outskirts of the city to pick some greens from a field. Food in Salonica was scarce at that time and people found edible plants wherever they could.

When Christina and her mother realised that Rachel had been sitting all alone in her room, they told her that their home was now her home and she should see it that way. They said that if she wakes up and no one is there,

---

[53] An emperor of Russia before 1917.

she should go to the kitchen and help herself to some milk and bread with honey.

For the rest of the day Rachel helped out with some chores. She also washed the wild greens in the sink and then placed them in a pot to boil. At six o'clock Father Nikolas arrived home. Rachel helped to set the table and had her second evening meal with Christina's family. After constant hunger in the ghetto, the wild greens tasted extra good. They were served with lots of olive oil and freshly squeezed lemon juice. There were also some fried sardines to go with the delicious greens. It was one of those meals that Rachel would never forget. Once she had helped with the washing up, she went into the sitting room where Father Nikolas was. A few minutes later, Christina came in. "Rachel we have something to tell you," she said.

"What is it?" asked Rachel.

"Your father's prayer shawl has to go," said Christina, "It's too dangerous to keep it here. If it's discovered, the Germans will arrest all of us."

"I'm sorry Rachel," said Father Nikolas, "But it's just too dangerous."

"But it looks like a scarf," said Rachel.

"Yes I agree with you," said the priest, "But not for the Germans. They know the difference between a prayer shawl and a scarf. My little one, you must understand something. The Jewish people are being hunted by the Germans. We cannot take this risk. We must burn it."

Rachel got up and went to her room. As she sat on her bed, she began to cry. Moments later, Christina came in. She sat down next to her and placed her arm around Rachel's shoulder.

"I'm really sorry that we have to do this," she said.

"It's just that it's been passed down from one generation to the next," said Rachel, "My great, great grandfather, purchased it in Constantinople[54] in the 1840s. It's one hundred years old and pure silk."

Rachel picked up the talit and handed it over to her friend.

"I also need your jacket with the yellow star," said Christina, "I'll remove the star, and burn it as well."

As Rachel handed the jacket over, Evangelia came in and hugged her. The whole family understood how difficult this was for her, and Rachel was beginning to understand how necessary it was to get rid of these items. Christina left the room and went into the kitchen where she placed both the prayer shawl and the yellow 'Star of David' into the wood-burning stove.

For the next four weeks, Rachel did not leave Christina's house. During the day, after helping with the basic chores, she was confined to her room where she worked on a crocheted tapestry. At the hacienda, Rachel had only learned embroidery, and this was her first attempt at crocheting. Christina's mother taught her this skill and she really enjoyed it. Her first creation was a cushion cover. This gave her a lot of confidence and so she set her mind to creating something bigger. Initially, she was going to make a small rug but it ended up becoming a large and colourful tapestry. By the

---

[54] Constantinople was the capital city of the Byzantine Empire (330-1453) and the later Ottoman Empire (1453-1923). The modern Turkish name for the city, Istanbul, derives from the Greek phrase "into the city".

end of the war when it was finally completed, it was so huge that it could be used as a quilt.

During those first few weeks at Christina's house, Rachel would often look out of her second floor window down onto the main street, feeling completely heartbroken. Around midday every second day, she could see a long line of people with their suitcases by their side slowly marching towards the railway station.

She knew that they were Jews and the ghetto of Salonica was being emptied. These people however, were not from the Baron Hirsch district ghetto. They were coming from the other side of Salonica and it took at least three and a half hours on foot to reach the railway station. As Rachel watched the elderly, the young, the lame and all the mothers carrying their toddlers, walking against the cold wind, a flood of tears ran down her face. Then in the evening, she would again weep as she heard the sound of the harmonica from downstairs. The ground floor of the building was occupied by another family who were well-known right-wing nationalists. The father and son would play the harmonica every evening. Rachel couldn't bear to hear the sound of the harmonica as it reminded her of her own brother Moishe. He was truly a gifted harmonica player, who flawlessly played all the Spanish tunes that he had learnt from his grandfather. The lyrics of these songs were in the Ladino language and many times Rachel would accompany her brother's playing with her beautiful singing. For as long as Rachel was at Christina's house, she would hear the sound of the harmonica which made her cry herself to sleep.

A month later, something good happened that was very liberating for Rachel. Father Nikolas was able to obtain false papers for Rachel from a black market underground operation. It cost him 25 drachmas which was a substantial amount at the time. Rachel insisted that she would pay him back the 25 drachmas after the war but he wouldn't hear of it.
"For me all human beings are an image of God," he told Rachel, "I am only doing what Christ would have done under the same circumstances." As the false papers were handed over to Rachel she immediately noticed that the photo was the same as the one on her old identity document but she had a brand new name and a different birthday.

The ID read:
Name: Maria Dimitriou Karidis
Father's Name: Dimitrios Apostolou Karidis
Mother's Name: Eleni Amanatidou Karidis
Place of Birth: Salonica, Greece
Date of Birth: 15 September 1923
Religion: Greek Orthodox Christian

The only thing that was accurate was Rachel's place of birth. She was told to memorize all the details on her new ID. Rachel did not sleep until the early hours of the morning as she was determined to memorize the details perfectly.

The following morning after breakfast, Christina asked Rachel to come into her room. Rachel was shown how to do the sign of the cross and together with her friend they read the Lord's Prayer over and over. Rachel was told to memorize it by the next day.

She did as she was instructed and the next day, just before going outside for a long awaited walk, Christina's mother placed a gold crucifix chain around Rachel's neck.

"As long as the Germans are in our country, you must never take this off," said Christina's mother, "And one day when the war is over, I don't want you to give it back, this is yours to keep."

Rachel hugged the priest's wife as tightly as she could. She could not believe how lucky she was to have such wonderful people looking after her.

Rachel really enjoyed her long strolls in the Salonican sun but going out was not without its risks. It was already mid-May and the weather had begun to warm up. After a few weeks in hiding, Christina's mother's sister paid them a visit. Rachel was not sure if she knew of her real identity and she did not ask.

Rachel and Christina's aunt really liked each other and got on well. That afternoon after enjoying a cup of coffee at her sister's house, she asked Rachel if she would like to go for a stroll to the White Tower.

"Yes, I would," replied Rachel.

They ambled along the avenue making idle chatter. Rachel was engrossed in their conversation when a man's voice from behind startled her. The man had a camera and wanted to take a picture of these two fine ladies. Christina's aunt immediately agreed and then once the photo was taken she gave the man her address and was to pay him upon delivery. Despite this entire incident being innocent, it traumatized Rachel because in reality she was still evading the Nazis, living under an assumed name and hiding in plain sight.

A few months later, at the end of August, another incident occurred that made Rachel very nervous. Rachel and Christina were out in the city centre one afternoon, not only to enjoy the glorious summer weather but also to see a movie at the theatre. The films that were being played during this time were mostly German and Italian. On that day they saw an Italian romance film set in the 19th century. After the film, they began to make their way back home, chatting about the film as they walked. They walked along Egnatia Avenue and as they passed the Arch of Galerius[55], a convoy of trucks drove up and stopped. At least fifty soldiers, if not more, jumped out of the trucks.

"Papiere, papiere[56]," yelled the soldiers.

Rachel and Christina hurriedly reached inside their handbags and took out their ID papers. A German soldier snatched them out of their hands and after a quick look, he threw the two pieces of paper back at them and the documents fell to the ground. The girls quickly bent down and picked

---

[55] A Roman monument built at the end of the 3rd century AD to honour the victories of the Emperor Galerius against the Persians in Asia Minor and Syria.
[56] *German* (Identification) Papers

them up all the while being screamed at and told to remain on the side along with others. As the minutes went by they saw people being pushed, shoved and hit. They were the lucky ones because anyone with no ID papers was shot on the spot. It took about half an hour for the situation to calm down. By this stage, Rachel and Christina had slowly made their way to the back of the crowd but they realised that they had been encircled. Everyone inside that circle was like a hostage. Christina sat on the ground pulling Rachel down with her. She whispered to Rachel to do whatever she did. Christina then slowly began to move backwards. Rachel did exactly the same. Directly behind them, there were no soldiers, only shrubs. Christina kept checking very carefully and continued moving backwards until she shoved her way right into the shrub. The others, who were being held involuntarily, were staring at the antics of the girls. Rachel took a quick look behind her and saw that Christina had disappeared into the shrub. She knew that it was now her turn. Before she had a chance to make another move, a very loud whistle blew. Whoever was sitting down stood up and they all began marching forward. Rachel had a strong feeling that if she was to stand up and go with all the others, the end result would not be good. She remained seated and made one big move backwards into the bushes. She felt someone's hands under her arms pulling her along and she knew that it was Christina. They remained hidden in the dried up bushes without making a sound. They had no idea whether or not they had been spotted. As the time passed they heard the other hostages being loaded onto trucks and the trucks drove away. Even when it all seemed clear, they still sat there looking out from the bushes onto the street.

Christina whispered to Rachel that they couldn't stay there all night, so once again she instructed her to follow her lead. They made her way out of the bushes on all fours. As they both stood up wiping away the shrubs from their arms, they found themselves face to face with a Greek policeman, who had been left there undoubtedly by the Germans. He motioned to them to leave.

"Quickly, go, go," he said.

Both girls began to hurry along.

"Don't run," warned the policeman.

They slowed down and eventually made their way back home. They never did find out why the Germans blocked the area that day, nor did they ever learn what had happened to the hostages.

Rachel had now been staying at Christina's house for five months. During this time, whenever they had visitors, she was always introduced as Christina's mother's niece who had come from the countryside and was staying with them for a while. This story was told to everyone - even to their neighbours downstairs who occasionally came up for a cup of coffee. They were well-known fascists but Christina's family had to pretend to like them as they shared the same apartment building. This family had gained notoriety in 1913 during the battle to reclaim Salonica from the Ottoman Turks. They had slaughtered their fellow Greeks who had hidden Turkish Muslim families in their homes during this time when chaos and lawlessness prevailed.

One morning in early September, Christina's mother got a visit from Mrs. Irini, her neighbour across the street, who told her something alarming. Apparently, their neighbours downstairs had suspected for a while that her so-called niece from the countryside was not her niece at all. They believed that this girl who had been staying with them was Jewish and that she was hiding at their house. Apparently, the only reason why they hadn't gone to the Gestapo with this piece of information was because the head of the household was an Orthodox priest. Mrs Irini was concerned that it was only a matter of time before they were betrayed to the Nazis. It was believed that they would collect a large amount of money for this sort of information.

"Take her away from here," said the neighbour, "You don't want the Germans to find her here. They will shoot all of you."

Rachel and Christina had spent that day at the Church. Rachel always helped out with anything that needed to be done. As soon as the girls arrived home, Christina's parents informed them of what Mrs. Irini had said.

"We have no time to waste," said Father Nikolas, "You must leave tonight under the cover of darkness."

Rachel stood there in shock, gently nodding her head.

"I'll go and get some of my things," she said.

"No," said the priest, "You must leave with no luggage, just as you are."

Christina was instructed by her father to take Rachel back to the Church, and to wait there in complete silence. Both girls left the house and quickly made their way to the Church. A few hours later, at approximately six o'clock, Father Nikolas arrived at the Church with a man who the girls did not know. After being introduced, the girls were told that he was to escort Rachel to her next hiding place.

"Don't be afraid," said the priest, "I trust this man with my life."

Rachel sat there with a blank look on her face, knowing that she had no other choice but to trust Father Nikolas' friend. After saying goodbye to Christina and the priest, she walked out of the Church into the quiet streets of Salonica with a complete stranger whom she had no option but to follow to an unknown destination.

CHAPTER FIVE

The Couple from the Black Sea

Rachel and her guide walked through the silent streets of Salonica constantly watching their backs. They crossed roads and they walked through side streets until they reached the nearest forest. The guide motioned for her to sit down. He told Rachel that they had been walking for two hours and they had another two hours to go. Rachel was very tired but she was too frightened to delay this journey so she did whatever he told her to do. Ten minutes later they got up and carried on walking. Two hours passed and once again they stopped. The tall stranger told Rachel to wait under a tree until his return. The guide came back a little while later with two donkeys. It was now close to midnight and Rachel could not believe that they had not yet reached their destination. She wanted to know where they were going but he refused to say. She pleaded with him to resume the journey in the morning. He said that where they were going was a long way away and that they must leave immediately. He told her that when she rode on the donkey she could sleep. Donkeys have a habit of following each other so there was no need for Rachel to keep her eyes open. For the next twelve hours Rachel was falling in and out of sleep on the back of the donkey. She was grateful that she didn't have to walk all that way.

The early morning light woke her as it touched her eyes but she continued to doze on and off until they reached their destination.

"We've arrived," said the guide as he nudged her arm.

He helped Rachel to climb off the donkey and she followed him into a tiny chapel. Rachel stood just inside the entrance as the guide approached the priest. Moments later the priest motioned for Rachel to follow them. They exited a side door and sat down at a table.

"You can't stay in Naousa," said the priest.

That's when Rachel realised where she was.

The priest said to the guide, "All of the hiding places have been taken, but don't worry. I will tell you where to take this poor soul."

As Rachel stared at the priest, he gave her a faint smile, "Don't be afraid. We will find a place for you to stay! It just can't be in Naousa."

The priest left the room and returned shortly after with bread, cheese, olives and retsina[57].

Despite not having eaten for at least a day, Rachel wasn't very hungry. Her stomach was in knots and she was unable to relax because of the uncertainty of her situation. After the meal, the priest asked Rachel to go into the chapel and take a seat.

"If a German soldier enters the chapel pretend to pray," he said as he left with the guide.

Rachel's heart stopped, and she began to pray fervently that no German soldier entered the chapel. She must have fallen asleep for she was awoken by a familiar voice.

"Come on Maria," said the guide, "We're on our way to Kozani."

---

[57] Greek wine flavoured with resin.

Rachel stood up and on her way out she kissed the priest's hand and thanked him profusely as he gave her a loaf of bread.

"May the Virgin Mary be with you," he said as Rachel and her guide mounted the donkeys and set off once again.

"How long will it take to get to Kozani?" she asked.

"At least fifteen hours," he replied, "We should be there by nine o'clock tomorrow morning."

"Couldn't we go anywhere closer?" she asked.

"I wanted to go to Edessa," said the guide, "It's only six hours away, but the priest doesn't know anyone there that he can trust. The family in Kozani that will take you in, he trusts with his life."

Throughout their journey to Kozani, they stopped only twice to share the bread and cheese that the priest had given them. The guide was careful to avoid all main roads and instead went through farmland, forests and along many ridges. They had to avoid creeks as donkeys don't like to cross water. It was a part of Greece that Rachel had never seen before and its beauty was so breathtaking that it left an indelible impression on her. Just as the guide had predicted, they finally arrived at their destination the following morning. Rachel remained on her donkey as her guide approached the house and knocked on the door. He then handed a letter over to the man of the house. Moments later, a rugged looking man approached Rachel.

"Come on my young one," he said, "You are more than welcome to stay at my home."

Rachel was helped down from the donkey and approached the house. The lady of the house came out and warmly welcomed her.

"Come in, come in," she said, "You can stay as long as you like. Father Elias's friends are always welcome in our home."

Rachel couldn't believe the kindness of these people. She was extremely grateful.

"So your name's Maria," said the friendly man.

Rachel nodded realising that her fake name was in the letter.

"My name is Vasili and my wife's name is Euthimia."

"It's very nice to meet you both," said Rachel as she held out her hand.

The couple ignored her outstretched hand but rather took turns in hugging her warmly and making her feel as welcome as they could.

Euthimia immediately filled the bath tub with hot water and handed Rachel a bar of soap and some new clothes to wear.

"When you finish washing, we will eat."

Rachel couldn't stop thanking her.

"It's nothing," said Euthimia, "Don't even think about it."

When Rachel came out of the small room behind the kitchen she noticed that her guide had left.

"He had to go," said Vasili, "He asked me to say goodbye to you."

Rachel smiled as she hesitantly sat down.

"Don't be shy," said Vasili, "For as long as you're here, treat this house as your own."

"Thank you, I will," replied Rachel.

"So you're from Salonica?" asked Vasili.

"Yes, I am," said Rachel, "And this is Kozani, is that right?"

"Actually, this is a little village just outside of Kozani. It's very quiet here, no one ever bothers us."

That evening Rachel once again felt safe. She was in the company of angels and before going to bed she made sure to thank her creator for her good fortune.

In the next few weeks, Rachel found herself slowly becoming more comfortable as she was getting used to living with this lovely couple. She got to know them well as they lived alone. Their five children were married and lived nearby with their own families.

Every evening after dinner, the three of them sat on the sofa and the couple took turns in telling Rachel about their traumatic escape from their hometown of Trapezounta.

"We're from the Euxine Pontus[58]," said Vasili, "Trapezounta had been our home for nearly three thousand years."

Vasili relayed to Rachel the stories that had been passed down from one generation to the next. Trapezounta was an ancient Greek colony that had been founded 2700 years ago.

It was located on the Black Sea with the famous Silk Road running through the city. For centuries it was at the epicentre of trade and commerce. The couple wept as they told Rachel how their families were involved in the textile industry and how they had worked hard for their success only to be deported from their own land twenty years earlier. They had fled with nothing but the clothes on their backs.

---

[58] The 'Euxine Pontus' is the Greco-Roman name for the Black Sea.

In 1923, the Greek, Turkish and British governments made a back room deal without considering the implications for the thousands upon thousands of lives that would be negatively impacted. They decided that, in order to solve the age old problem of territorial rights between Greece and Turkey, the first thing that needed to be done was an exchange of population. The entire Christian population of Turkey, which primarily consisted of Greeks, was to uproot and move back to their ancestral homeland of Greece. Likewise, the Muslim population of Greece was to move to Turkey.

"We lost everything," said Euthimia, "We arrived here with nothing. The Greek government had set up tents for the refugees but there were so many people that three families had to share one tent. We had five children below the age of ten. Can you imagine the hell we went through?"

"When did you move into this house?" asked Rachel.

"When I built it, fifteen years ago," replied Vasili, "I'm a builder and I also built my children's houses."

"Are people still living in those tents?" asked Rachel.

"No," replied Vasili, "The last tent came down eight years ago."

That evening as Rachel lay down to sleep, she thought of her own family and where on earth could they be. She knew that they had been taken to Germany but did not know anything more. In the meantime, she could only pray that they were alive somewhere in the world. She hoped that one day in the near future they would be able to live together in their own

Jewish ancestral homeland and never have to withstand foreign powers dictating their fate.

Living at Vasili and Euthimia's house was typical country living, which Rachel hadn't experienced before. The closest she came to that lifestyle was spending holidays at her family's bungalow on the Kassandra coast for eight weeks during the summer. This however was different because there was no sea, just acres and acres of farmland. All of Vasili and Euthimia's neighbours were refugees who had come to Kozani in 1923. They were so bonded that they all shared the milk, the bread and everything else. They even shared the produce from their vegetable patches. Every day Rachel helped Euthimia with the cooking and cleaning and on occasion she helped out the other villagers with their planting. Most of that autumn, she mainly helped with the picking of olives from the many olive trees in the area.

She had been introduced to the other villagers as a relative of Euthimia's and since she looked very much like the Anatolian Greeks, she was able to blend in.

"You look 100% Pontian[59]," said a neighbour.

"Of course she does," replied Euthimia, "She's my cousin's daughter."

Rachel never asked Vasili and Euthimia why she was introduced as a relative. Nor did she ask them if they knew of her real identity. Eventually however, during her stay, she was to learn the answer under the most stressful circumstances.

---

[59] The Pontian Greeks are an ethnically Greek group who traditionally lived on the shores of the Black Sea and the Pontic Mountains of north-eastern Anatolia.

Three weeks into Rachel's stay with Vasili and Euthimia, she received an unexpected visitor. Christina had come to Kozani for a week. As soon as Rachel saw her she dropped whatever she was doing and hugged her very tightly.

"I can't believe you're here," said Rachel.

"You left us so unexpectedly that I had to come and see you."

"How are your parents and sister?" asked Rachel.

"They send their love," replied Christina, "Here! I have a present for you." She then revealed the tapestry crochet that Rachel had been working on in Salonica.

"I've actually missed it," said Rachel, "Thank you for bringing it to me."

"You're most welcome," said Christina.

For the next few days Christina and Rachel had a lot of catching up to do. She explained everything that had transpired in Salonica after Rachel had left. Two days after Rachel's sudden departure, the Gestapo had come to their apartment with two soldiers. The Gestapo stood there as the soldiers searched every room and wardrobe. They then left without saying a word about why they were there. Christina's family could only guess that the people downstairs had said something to the German authorities. Christina explained to Rachel that if and when she does return to Salonica she won't be able to hide in their home. She told her to have patience until they could find a hiding place for her somewhere in Salonica. Rachel of course sang the praises of her dear hosts and explained how happy she was. This contentment that Rachel was feeling however, had to do with an ethereal presence that was surrounding her. This was something that had first transpired when she was a child. She opened up to Christina and told her of this secret that she had never divulged to anyone before.

One hot summer evening, at the age of seven, Rachel saw an angel in the courtyard of the hacienda. It was in human form wearing white robes and it appeared to have wings. She began to yell at the top of her lungs, "There's someone in the courtyard."

Her parents searched everywhere but found nothing. They told her that it was probably just her imagination. However, Rachel knew that it wasn't. For the next three years, the angel appeared before her four more times. She had learned her lesson and did not reveal this to anyone. By the time she had her last encounter, she knew that it was her own guardian angel that was constantly watching over her. In Kozani, despite never seeing the angel, she constantly felt its presence. She felt she was able to share this with her best friend for the first time.

Seven days later, when it was time for Christina to leave, both girls embraced not wanting to let go. On one hand, Rachel felt sad because her best friend had to go back to Salonica but on the other hand, she was very happy living with Vasili and Euthimia.

A few weeks later, Rachel was introduced to Sophia, a young newly-wed who was a couple of years older than Rachel. She lived in the neighbouring village and wasn't a refugee. Her family had been in Kozani since the days of Alexander the Great and they considered themselves the true natives of this land. The girls started up a friendship and they began spending a lot of time together, especially in the kitchen. Rachel would visit her often and she sat in the kitchen as Sophia cooked. One day Sophia had just killed one of her chickens and after plucking it she cut it up and placed it in her cooking pot half-filled with water. To Rachel's surprise, she then added 12 saffron threads, a teaspoon of paprika and half a cup of olive oil. She brought the liquid to a boil and left it to simmer.

"I haven't slaughtered a chicken in a while," said Sophia, "I'm very careful to use up what we already have before slaughtering anything new. This war seems never ending and only God knows how long this depression will last for."

"What is the dish that you're making?" asked Rachel.

"It's called Kozani chicken," she replied.

"I saw that you added saffron threads," said Rachel.

"Saffron is *the* spice of Kozani," said Sophia, "We cook most of our meals with saffron."

"My mother used saffron as well," said Rachel, "However, I'm not sure if she cooked chicken with saffron."

"For what dishes did she use saffron?" asked Sophia.

"For all the fish dishes," replied Rachel, "Especially during pascha[60]. The fish is baked in the oven with saffron, paprika and green peppers."

"Don't you have lamb?" asked Sophia, "Here in Kozani eating lamb has become a ritual on Easter Sunday."

Rachel's stomach tightened in a painful knot. She had made a colossal slip. How could she have done that? She immediately tried to fix it.

---

[60] The Greek word for Easter and Passover.

"Well my grandmother is from Spain and during pascha the Spaniards have fish instead of lamb."

The truth was that Rachel had no idea what the Spanish Christians had during Easter. All she knew was what the Spanish Jews had traditionally eaten for centuries during Passover. She sat there and looked at Sophia hoping that she asks no more questions. To her relief Sophia changed the subject by asking Rachel to come to her bedroom to show her the beautiful quilt that she used as a bedspread.

"This quilt belonged to my grandmother," said Sophia, "My mother gave it to me on my wedding day."

On her way back to Vasili and Euthimia's house, she could not stop scolding herself. She did not know how she could have slipped up like that. Her mistake took its toll on her mentally as she began living day to day with fear and paranoia. For the rest of her stay in Kozani, Rachel never visited Sophia again. She spent most of her days within the safe walls of Vasili and Euthimia's home.

Three and a half months into Rachel's stay at Kozani, an event occurred that traumatized the entire village. It was a bitterly cold Sunday morning in January. Rachel was at home preparing the salad for Sunday lunch with Vasili and Euthimia. She did this every Sunday when Vasili and Euthimia were at Church. Through the kitchen window she saw German soldiers driving by in cars. Her knees began to wobble. She had not seen one German soldier since she arrived in Kozani. She did not know what to make of it.

Vasili and Euthimia arrived home from church and Rachel immediately told them what she had seen. They had not seen anything.

They sat down and had their simple lunch. Olives and lettuce salad, fried eggplants and some bread. As they were eating and making idle chatter, their neighbour's grandson Jordan came running into their house.

"The Germans are here! They're searching all the houses."

"Why?" asked Vasili.

"Because in the neighbouring town, some people were hiding Jews."

"And what happened?"

"They were all executed this morning."

The young boy quickly ran out and left behind three people who were frozen with fear. Vasili told Rachel that he and his wife knew that she was Jewish. He told her not to worry but that it would be best that she remained hidden when the Germans arrived.

"But I have fake ID papers," she said.

"So did the Jewish couple in the neighbouring village."

Rachel then realised that Vasili and Euthimia not only knew of the doomed family in the neighbouring village but also that they had been hiding Jews.

She immediately obeyed as Euthimia and Vasili took her into their bedroom and opened up the wardrobe door.

"You will hide up there," said Vasili.

It was a late nineteenth century closet. The shelf height and depth were only twenty inches, but horizontally there was a long space that went from one end of the wardrobe to the other. For a moment Rachel pondered whether or not she would be able to fit but she soon found herself stepping onto the chair and attempted to climb into that small space. Euthimia and Vasili were trying to push her in. After somewhat of a struggle, Rachel finally made it. She was lying down on her tummy.

"It's better to lie on your back," said Euthimia.

With some difficulty, Rachel slowly rolled over until she was lying on her back. Euthimia stood on the chair as Vasili handed her a thick woven blanket. She spread it across the shelf, right on top of Rachel.

"Can you breathe?" she asked.

"Yes," replied Rachel.

"Don't move until we come back for you."

Rachel lay there in Euthimia's closet beneath the thick blanket and waited patiently with her heart beating rapidly.

About an hour later, just as Rachel had drifted off to sleep, there was a loud bang on the door. Rachel's heart leapt and she was so nervous that she became numb. She couldn't believe that it had come to this. There were three Germans who came into the house. The senior officer stayed in the living room with Vasili and Euthimia who stood nervously to attention. The other two soldiers searched the entire house. As Rachel lay there in silence she heard the sounds of footsteps in the couple's bedroom. The soldier opened all the bedside draws and then came over to the closet. He opened it up and began shuffling through the coat hangers. He then removed all the blankets and other items that were on the bottom of the closet. This search took less than two minutes but for Rachel it seemed like two hours. She held her breath as she prayed to God in silence. The soldier left the room and within minutes the three Germans had left the house.

Vasili and Euthimia did not come to bring Rachel down from her hiding place until late in the evening when the word had spread that the Germans had left the village. Once Rachel came out of hiding, Euthimia told her that from then on she was never to leave her room, even during meal times.

"It's not safe here anymore," said Vasili, "We will get in touch with Father Nikolas in Salonica to see if they have found a hiding place for you there."

Rachel apologized profusely. She felt guilty for having to put Vasili and Euthimia at risk.

"It's not your fault," said Euthimia, "We would do this all over again if we had to."

In the next few days, Rachel was to learn that the family in the neighbouring village who had hidden Jews were Sophia's aunt and uncle. They, together with the Jewish couple, were executed outside of their home in the early hours of that fateful Sunday.

Rachel was now more terrified than ever. She did not dare to leave her bedroom. She just crocheted her tapestry and waited patiently for word from Salonica where she longed to return.

CHAPTER SIX

The Final Hiding Place

In the coming weeks, Rachel did as Vasili and Euthimia had instructed her to - she remained in her bedroom. Euthimia had even gone as far as to place a bed pan in her room.

"Don't be embarrassed," she said, "I will empty it every day."

But Rachel was really embarrassed. She only began using the bed pan after a day and a half when her bladder was about to burst.

One evening, Euthimia came to Rachel's room and sat on her bed. She comforted her and assured her everything would be alright. Rachel had a million questions for her but only mustered up the courage to ask her just one.

"Mrs. Euthimia, may I please ask you something?" she asked as she sat in her bed with her night gown on.

"Of course you can," replied Euthimia.

"Now that I'm confined to my bedroom, does that mean I won't be able to have a bath?"

"My dear girl," said Euthimia, "Of course you can have a bath. But it's better to have one in the evening. Tomorrow we will discuss it further."

The following day, just as Euthimia had promised, she went into Rachel's bedroom and they discussed the bathing details. That evening Euthimia filled the bath tub with warm water and placed a bar of soap beside it.

"Rachel," she said as she opened the bedroom door, "Come, the bath tub is waiting for you."

Rachel went into the laundry room at the back of the house. She removed all her clothes and she gently slid into the bath tub. As she washed herself, she thought about Vasili and Euthimia. What wonderful people they were and how blessed she was to have come into contact with them. They were truly sent by God.

Three weeks later, just when Rachel was beginning to feel restless and uncertain, she had an unexpected visitor. One afternoon as she lay on her bed there was a knock on her door. The door opened slightly and Christina's sister, Evangelia, stood there smiling. Rachel leapt to her feet and threw her arms around her.

"I can't believe you're here," said Rachel.

"I've come to take you back to Salonica," she said, "Are you ready to go?"

"Right now?" asked Rachel.

"Yes, right now," replied Evangelia.

Rachel had so many questions to ask but she knew that she would be able to ask these things during their journey back. She began placing the few items that she had into her small suitcase that Christina had dropped off five months earlier.

"Don't forget this," said Evangelia as she held the tapestry in her hand. Rachel placed it carefully on top of her meagre belongings and closed the suitcase.

The girls were to be escorted by Vasili to the closest railway station. Once Rachel had helped Vasili load her suitcase onto the donkey. She turned to

Euthimia and hugged her. They both cried and remained in a tight embrace, neither wanting to let go first. Rachel, Evangelia and Vasili each mounted a donkey and they began their one hour journey to the railway station in Kozani. When they arrived at the station, Evangelia purchased the train tickets and the three of them sat on a bench and waited in silence for the train. When the train arrived, Rachel and Vasili hugged, "I want to thank you for everything," said Rachel as Vasili's eyes welled up.

The girls boarded the train and Rachel waved a tearful goodbye to Vasili, leaning far out of the window as the train left the station. Rachel continued to wave until Vasili was no longer visible. Rachel sat in her seat next to Evangelia but she remained silent for the 45 minute journey to Veria. She was unable to speak. She felt heartbroken as though she had said goodbye to her parents for the last time. Once in Veria, the girls got off the train and waited on the platform for the connecting train that would take them straight to Salonica. Within an hour the train arrived and Rachel and Evangelia boarded. Once they found their allocated seats they sat and waited for the train to leave. There seemed to be a delay and it soon became evident why. They looked out of the window and noticed a large number of German soldiers boarding the train.

"Try not to appear nervous," said Evangelia.

Rachel remained silent as she waited for the train to begin moving.

"How long till we get to Salonica?" she finally asked.

"We should be there in an hour," replied Evangelia.

Rachel was surprised at how short the trip was.

"When I came to Kozani five months ago, why didn't I come by train?" she asked.

"It was too dangerous," replied Evangelia.

"It took us forever to get to Vasili and Euthimia's house," said Rachel.

Evangelia nodded and smiled as she placed her arm around Rachel.

Much to their relief, all the German soldiers got off the train at a stop about twenty minutes into the journey.

"Now we can at least breathe," said Evangelia.

Rachel smiled as she moved a bit closer to her friend, "You haven't told me where you're taking me," she whispered.

Evangelia then reached inside her hand bag and produced a small piece of paper.

"I've been instructed to take you to this address," she said as she handed the note to Rachel.

As she gazed down at the paper she instantly recognised the address. It was where her dear friend Stella lived.

"This is my friend's house," she said.

Evangelia looked at her, puzzled.

"Is it?" she asked.

"Yes," replied Rachel, "She is the woman who is partly deaf."

"But isn't she Jewish?" asked Evangelia.

"Yes she is, but her husband is Italian."

"Well then that explains it," said Evangelia, "She probably has immunity."

"Probably," said Rachel.

A short while later the train arrived at Salonica railway station. Rachel and Evangelia got off the train with their cases and began the long walk towards the port. Half an hour later, Rachel spotted the White Tower from a distance and noticed the Nazi flag on top of the tower, waving in the wind. Despite this painful sight, Rachel felt safe because she had arrived home. She was familiar with all her surroundings and as they got ever closer, she led the way to Stella's house.

They arrived at the front door and Rachel pressed the doorbell.

"Who is it?" said a soft spoken voice through the intercom.

"Maria, the Italian girl," replied Evangelia.

Rachel stared at her friend, quickly realising that she had been instructed to say this. The buzzer sounded and both girls pushed the door open. They took the elevator to the top floor where Stella was waiting for them. Rachel embraced her dear friend and they walked arm in arm into the apartment. Stella's daughters were there to greet her and Rachel hugged them tightly, "They have grown so much," she said.

For the rest of the evening she told Stella about the ghetto and how her family had been deported to Germany.

"You're very lucky to have friends like Christina and Evangelia," said Stella.

"We love Rache… I mean Maria," said Evangelia, "There isn't much that we wouldn't do for her."

Evangelia left to go home and Stella escorted Rachel to her new bedroom.

"This is a very big room," said Rachel.

"It's all yours," she said as she went ahead and showed her the adjoining bathroom.

"I can't believe this," said Rachel, "I've never had my own bathroom. How can I ever repay you?"

"You're forgetting that I'm Jewish too," replied Stella, "How can I not help you?"

"Why weren't you deported?" asked Rachel.

"It's a long story," said Stella, "Unpack, take a bath and then if you're not too tired I will tell you all about it."

Rachel did just that. She immersed herself in the warm water, only to fall asleep. The bath water grew cold and Rachel woke up with a start. She went straight to bed, too tired to talk to Stella.

The following day breakfast was served on the glass-enclosed patio. Rachel felt as though they were eating outside. For the rest of the day, Stella and Rachel caught up on all their news. Stella explained that Christina had come to her apartment a few months earlier and had asked for her help. Only then did Rachel remember telling Christina about Stella.

"As soon as your friend Christina told me that you needed a place to stay, I immediately said you should come."

"What about your husband?" asked Rachel, "Is he okay with it?"

"Of course he is," replied Stella, "He agreed to it but only under one condition."

"Which is?" asked Rachel.

"That you pose as an Italian citizen."

"How do I do that?"

"Firstly, knowledge of the language, which I know isn't a problem as you speak Italian."

Rachel nodded as she thought back to her student days when she always came first in her Latin and Italian classes.

"Secondly, you need a brand new identity."

"Not another one," said Rachel.

"Don't worry," said Stella, "Your Christian name stays the same."

Stella handed Rachel her new ID papers.

"Here they are," she said, "I didn't tell you yesterday because I didn't want to overwhelm you."

Rachel looked down at her new identity. She was listed as Maria Vittoria Agati.

"You need to memorize all the particulars and you need to carry them with you wherever you go," said Stella.

"What about my Greek ID?"

"Get rid of it."

"Alright, I'll burn it tonight," said Rachel.

"There's one more thing that I need to show you," said Stella.

"What's that?" asked Rachel.

"From now on, this is how you do the sign of the cross. When you cross yourself, you go from your left shoulder to your right shoulder."

Rachel stared at her friend in disbelief.

"Don't worry," said Stella, "I'm also posing as a Roman Catholic. I will teach you everything you need to know."

That afternoon, Rachel and Stella sat in the living room sipping their chamomile infused tea. Stella told Rachel how her husband was unable to obtain immunity for his wife and two children, despite being a member of Italy's Fascist Party. He saved them by obtaining fake papers for Stella and his daughters at the last minute.

"For the girls as well?" asked Rachel.

"Half-Jews are not exempt," said Stella, "The Nazis are deporting all Jews even those with one Jewish grandparent."

"When did you receive your fake ID?" asked Rachel.

"In October of last year," she replied.

Stella then went on to explain how the previous summer was the most uncertain time of all. The Duce[61], was voted out of power by his own Grand Council in July of 1943. Then in early September, Italy surrendered to the Allies. This was the worst time for Stella's family. If it wasn't for her husband's close ties with a top Nazi official in Salonica, the whole family would have been arrested but instead they were allowed to stay without any problems.

"So that is how you managed to stay in Salonica without being arrested," said Rachel.

"Yes, that is how," replied Stella.

"How about your parents, are they still in Salonica?"

"Oh no," replied Stella, "They're in Switzerland."

---

[61] **Benito Mussolini was identified as** *Il Duce* **(The Leader) of the Italian Fascist movement.**

Stella then told Rachel of the terrible ordeal her parents had gone through in September. Being Greek Jews they were in danger as all Jews were when the Nazis invaded Salonica in 1941. However, because their son-in-law was an Italian Baron he had influence and power and they managed to avoid being deported. They did, however, feel very vulnerable. One evening there was a knock at their door. It was the Gestapo. They were told that they had five minutes to pack a small case. When Stella's father asked the Gestapo where they were going, he was told that they were going to go on a long journey. They were taken to the police station where they waited for one day before their Italian son-in-law arrived to help them.

Stella recalled how one evening they were visited by her husband's German friend. He revealed to them that Stella's parents had been arrested but he also said that he had an idea. Her husband then left with the German Official and they went to the house of a Swiss consulate official who issued two Swiss visas for Stella's parents. Stella's husband went immediately to the police station where his in-laws were released. Instead of taking them home, he took them directly to the railway station. They waited for at least eight hours before boarding a train to Zurich, Switzerland. The Baron later confessed to his wife that when he walked into the police station that day he was fully aware that there were no guarantees that his in-laws would be released.

An entire week went by before Rachel met Stella's husband as he had been in Athens. He was what she expected a Baron to look like. He was tall, dark and handsome. He was extremely polite and he conversed with her in Italian. He even complimented her on how well she had mastered the Italian language. However, she was always nervous around him and avoided him whenever she could. He was a kind man but his regal bearing made Rachel feel uncomfortable. Whenever he was in Salonica she would usually only see him during dinner time.

As the weeks went by, Rachel bonded with Stella's daughters and she eventually became their private tutor. She taught them Greek History, Latin and Ancient Greek. She preferred to stay indoors and avoided going out unless Stella insisted. They would go to coffee shops and to the theatre. As they strolled along the streets of Salonica, Rachel was full of nostalgia. She remembered the not too distant days gone by which somehow felt so long ago. On one of their walks, Stella told Rachel about a party that she was going to hold at her house, at her husband's insistence. She said that Rachel must attend and that they should find her an evening gown for the occasion. Rachel was very reluctant but didn't argue too much because she didn't want to hurt Stella's feelings. There were only four stores with women's clothes open in Salonica, a far cry from the many that existed before the war. After looking at the dresses and not finding even one to try on, Stella decided that she was going to have one made especially for Rachel. That evening, Rachel mustered the strength to say emphatically that she did not want to attend the party. Stella seemed to understand and spoke of it no more, until the day of the party.

"Rachel I want to update you about this evening," she said, "The guests will begin to arrive at seven o'clock."

"Thanks for letting me know," said Rachel, "I will make myself scarce."

"I take it you still don't want to attend," said Stella.

Rachel shook her head.

"But I do have a question for you," said Rachel.

"Are there any Germans coming?"

"Yes, there are," Stella replied.

"Aren't you scared?" asked Rachel.

"They're my husband's friends and they don't know I'm Jewish... well except for one friend."

"Is he the friend who helped save your parents?"

"Yes," she replied.

Stella told Rachel that there would only be a few Germans as most of the guests were Diplomats from the neutral consulates that were still in Salonica.

That evening, Rachel sat quietly in her room. She heard the doorbell ringing continuously until all the visitors had arrived. Then the music began. The gramophone was on very loud and the first few songs were Greek, sung by Rachel's favourite singer, Sophia Vebo, whose voice echoed throughout the house. This was just too tempting for her as she got up from her bed walked to the door and opened it slowly. She tiptoed to the wooden stair banister and crouched down. She stared down at all the couples who danced to all of her favourite songs. She saw Stella dancing with the Baron. Rachel admired the women who looked so good in their

beautiful dresses and jewellery. For Rachel it was like watching a film except this was in colour and taking place right before her very eyes. Rachel was so envious as she stared down at the couples dancing. She was now twenty-one years of age and for the first time ever she wished that she could be married. Eventually, the Greek music was replaced with Italian songs. She stood up and walked quietly back to her room. She lay on her bed and listened to the music that continued to play downstairs.
That night she cried herself to sleep.

CHAPTER SEVEN

On A Mission

The days seemed to go by very fast for Rachel as she continued living with Stella's family.

"I can't believe that June is here already," said Rachel one morning during breakfast, "It was May Day only yesterday."

"I know my dear," said Stella "One day we'll wake up and be old ladies."

"Please don't say that," said Rachel, "I'm not married yet."

"Don't worry you soon will be," said Stella.

Rachel often struggled to understand what Stella was saying. Whenever she could, Stella used sign language to express herself.

Rachel went into the parlour where there was a lovely view of the back garden. The sun was shining brightly and she had a sudden urge to visit her friend Christina.

"It's turning out to be a beautiful day," said Rachel, "I'm going to visit my friend for a couple of hours."

"Alright," said Stella, "But take a cardigan with you. Summer hasn't exactly arrived yet."

Rachel took her dark green cardigan that was hanging on the coat hook. She blew a kiss to Stella as she left. She made her way down the usual side streets, even though it was now easier to avoid the Germans as one third of the German army had already withdrawn from the city of Salonica in April. When Rachel arrived at Christina's front door, she knocked softly as she didn't want the neighbours to hear anything. The door slowly opened and Evangelia peered out. She motioned for Rachel to enter. They greeted each other warmly with a kiss on the cheek. When Rachel entered the lounge room, she found the family sitting there. They all looked very sad and Christina's mother was holding a handkerchief and crying.

"What's the matter?" asked Rachel.

Christina stood up and went over and kissed her friend, "Come and take a seat, and we'll tell you all about it."

Rachel heard how Christina's mother's brother had been arrested by the Germans the day before. As far as they knew he had been taken to the Pavlos Melas camp[62] which was situated approximately four kilometres away on the outskirts of Salonica.

"Why was he arrested?" asked Rachel.

"Because he was involved with the resistance," replied Christina.

"So he was betrayed?"

"Not deliberately," replied Father Nikolas, "I believe his name was given to the Germans by someone who was being tortured."

"We have to do something," said Christina's mother, "There must be a way that we can get him out of there."

"I told you," said the priest, "Our only hope is to get in touch with our contact man in Serres."

Rachel felt very sad as she saw the agony evident in Christina's mother. She had met the uncle only once and she thought he was a polite, elegant

---

[62] This was an Ottoman Military Camp before the Greek army took over in 1912. They renamed it 'Pavlos Melas' camp, after the Greek war hero. In 1941, the Nazi occupiers turned it into a concentration camp.

gentleman. It would be an unimaginable tragedy for the family if they lost him. There was a knock on the door. Evangelia went to the front door. A man walked into the room and he stared at Rachel.

"Don't worry," said Father Nikolas, "She's one of ours."

"This is my friend Rachel," said Christina.

The young man introduced himself as Yianni Triantis. He was a member of the resistance and he explained that his relative is one of the guards at the Pavlos Melas camp. The camp was guarded entirely by Greeks who had right-wing political leanings. They could be bribed or in some cases they released prisoners as a favour to relatives. The only prisoners they never released were those who were left-wing affiliated – not even for a generous bribe.

"How soon can you make contact with your relative?" asked Christina. He went on to say that his contact man in Serres could get word to the guard in the camp within a week. However, his biggest obstacle was finding someone to get past the check points.

"Why's that?" asked Evangelia.

"Because the Greeks are not allowed through," replied Yianni, "The Germans are convinced that the civilian population is helping the guerrillas who are hiding out in the mountains."

"They'll let me through," said Rachel, "I have an Italian ID."

They all stared at Rachel in disbelief and then one by one began trying to convince her as to why it would be too dangerous for her to attempt this journey.

Rachel was not about to give in. She loved Christina's family and was so grateful for their kindness that she insisted on going.

"I am going whether you like it or not," she said in a loud, firm voice

"But Italy is no longer Germany's ally," said Christina, "I'm not sure if your Italian ID can be useful."

Then Yianni Triantis asked to see Rachel's ID. After close examination he read out aloud what was written on the ID paper,

"Name: Maria Vittoria Agati

Place of Birth: Rome, Italy

Date of Birth: 15 September 1923

Religion: Roman Catholic."

"What do you think?" asked the priest.

"It should work," he replied, "Anyone with foreign papers is not a suspect."

"Does that mean I can go?" asked Rachel.

After a moment's silence, "Yes," replied Yianni.

"Kai o Theos voithos[63]," said Father Nikolas.

Once it had been decided that Rachel would make the journey to Serres, they did not waste any more time. They immediately prepared a small backpack with some bread, cheese and honey. There were also two miniature glass bottles in the backpack. One was filled with retsina[64] and the other one with olive oil. Rachel removed the two bottles and said that it made the satchel too heavy. But to everyone's insistence she put them

---

[63] *Greek* with God's guidance and assistance.
[64] Greek wine flavoured with resin.

back into her small travel bag. They handed her a box of matches and asked her to open it. Underneath the matches there was a tiny map of eastern Macedonia. The monastery was marked with a red cross. It was located deep in the foothills of a mountainous range in southern Serres. It was 70 kilometres north-east of Salonica and it would take a good seven hours to get there by bicycle.

Rachel had to go to Father Nikolas' church to receive further instructions. During the next half hour they all left the apartment, two by two and in ten minute intervals so that their neighbours wouldn't be suspicious. Once they had all gathered at the Church, Yianni produced an envelope.

"Hide this letter in your petticoat," he said, "And when you arrive at the monastery, hand it over to Savva Iliadis. You must not give this to anyone else."

Evangelia offered Rachel some last minute advice.

"You must wind your wrist watch once a day as you can't afford to lose track of time during your journey."

Rachel nodded before looking at Christina, "Don't forget to tell Stella that I won't be home for a few days."

"Don't worry, I will go and tell her immediately."

"If you follow the directions on the map you shouldn't have any problems reaching the monastery before nightfall," said Yianni.

"Thank you my angel," said the priest's wife, "May the Virgin Mary protect you."

"It's already half past eleven," said Father Nikolas, "We mustn't hold her up any longer."

Rachel hugged everyone before mounting Christina's bicycle. She waved at them as she rode off on this very important mission.

As she cycled along under the warm sun, she passed many coffee shops and saw people sitting down enjoying their refreshments. It was late spring and the streets were full of people full of anticipation for the arrival of summer. After a short ride, Rachel saw a sign that read, 'STAVROUPOLI'. It was a suburb on the outskirts of the city of Salonica. She knew she was close to the 'Pavlos Melas' camp as it was situated in that town. Soon she saw the barbed wire fence and she instantly had a flashback to the previous year when she was incarcerated in the Baron Hirsch district ghetto. Whenever she thought of her escape, it sent chills up her spine. The memory was traumatic and she tried very hard not to think about it. It stuck Rachel as ironic that she needed to travel 70 kilometres in order to locate someone who had access to the Pavlos Melas camp which was only four kilometres from the city of Salonica.

Once she was clear of the city of Salonica she came across the first check point. She made every effort not to appear nervous. As she approached she got off her bike and handed her ID paper to the German soldier who was on guard. He looked carefully at the photograph before looking at Rachel. He then handed the ID paper back to her and he said, "Ciao[65] Maria," before laughing out loud.

"Ciao," said Rachel as she waved back at him.

---

[65] *Italian* Used as a greeting at meeting or parting: hello; goodbye; so long; see you later.

A while later Rachel stopped to check the map again. She also remembered to keep an eye on the time. It was half past three. She removed the map from the matchbox and studied it intently. She was somewhat confused because she had passed a number of towns which were not on the map. She then got back on her bike and continued cycling for another half an hour. She began encountering many ridges and creeks which looked familiar to her. It seemed to Rachel that it was the same beautiful area that she had gone through the previous autumn when she was on her way to Kozani on a donkey. Had she taken a wrong turn and gone in the opposite direction? She was not sure. She simply sensed that the monastery was a long way off. Rachel decided to ask the first person she came across for directions even though she had been instructed not to talk to anyone. However, she felt desperate as she had a strong feeling that she was lost. Rachel saw a priest walking along the side of the road up ahead. She approached him and asked for directions to the monastery in Serres.

He told her that she had taken a wrong turn five kilometres back. He told her that there was no point in continuing because she wouldn't get there before curfew time. He kindly offered to put her up for the evening at his house where he lived with his wife. Rachel knew that this was not part of the plan but felt like she had no choice. She knew that the priest was right. There was no way that she would reach Serres before nightfall so she accepted his generous offer.

When they reached the priest's house, his wife was extremely hospitable. She was very extroverted and could not stop talking. In Rachel's eyes it seemed as though she longed for company. Rachel helped with dinner preparations by washing the wild greens and putting them in a pot to boil. As an accompaniment there were a few things like black olives, feta cheese, pickled sardines, roasted peppers and fried eggplant. They told Rachel that they grew everything themselves, except for the pickled sardines that they had kept in their pantry for over a year. They said that it was the perfect time to open the jar of sardines because they had a dinner guest. Later that evening the priest's wife made the bed in the spare bedroom. Rachel thanked her profusely before lying down on the soft mattress. Before she knew it, she was fast asleep.

The following morning Rachel had breakfast with the couple. She had a warm cup of milk with bread and honey. Then before leaving she reached into her satchel and took out the two miniature bottles of retsina and olive oil. She left them both on the table. The priest and his wife protested loudly, demanding that she take them back. Rachel just smiled and waved to them before hurriedly continuing her journey. The priest's wife picked up the bottles and chased after Rachel but to no avail as she had disappeared into the distance.

Rachel rode her bike all the way back to where she missed the turning point. She continued to ride for another half an hour before stopping at a check point. There were four German soldiers at the barrier, who were very unfriendly. One of them looked at her ID paper as another emptied her satchel onto the ground. The match box fell out and Rachel was praying that they didn't open it. She was told to pack her things again. She approached the soldier who was holding her ID paper and he said to her in perfect Italian, "Why are you in Greece?"

She explained that she was staying with an Italian Baron in Salonica who happened to be a family friend. She said that she wanted to explore the Macedonian forest for a few days before returning to Salonica. He handed her ID back to her and motioned for her to go. Rachel continued riding for at least forty-five minutes before she came across a chaotic scene. She saw people running towards her and others falling to the ground as the sound of machine gun fire echoed around her. She saw German soldiers up ahead shooting at a line of people who had their hands up in the air. Rachel made a sharp right turn and as she rode into the bushes her bicycle hit a huge rock. Before she knew it she had fallen down the hillside with her bike tumbling after her.

As she lay there in shock, Rachel began to cry. She was feeling nervous and very anxious. She slowly got to her feet and picked up her bicycle. One of the metal bars had buckled but the bicycle was still rideable. However, she decided not to ride the bike. For the rest of that day she pushed her bike along in the Macedonian woods, avoiding the main road. When nightfall came she sat down under a tree. The shock of her experience that day unnerved her and she began to cry again until she fell into a fitful sleep.

It was daybreak when Rachel awoke. She was shivering and frozen to the bone. She slowly got up and was in desperate need to empty her bladder. She relieved herself under the tree. It was now her third day on the road and she was determined to find the monastery that day. Rachel swung her satchel onto her back and pushed her bike to the main road, where she mounted it and rode off. It wasn't long before she found herself riding past the dead bodies of the people who had been executed the previous day. She looked away and prayed not to come across any German soldiers. She continued to ride for about an hour when in the distance she saw a crucifix, visible over the top of the trees in the forest. As she got closer she saw that it was a monastery. Rachel became anxious, worried that it was not the right monastery. She stopped cycling and reached into her bag for the matchbox. She looked at the map one more time. She knew that she was in the right area so she continued riding. Half an hour later she reached a steep hill. Exhausted and unable to face riding up the hill, Rachel got off and pushed her bike.

She finally reached the monastery. She walked across the Chapel yard which had an olive tree in the centre. She looked around and saw a monk coming towards her.

"How can I help you?" he asked.

"I'm here to see Savva Iliadis," she replied, "I have a message for him."

"Follow me," said the monk.

Rachel breathed a sigh of relief that she was at the right monastery and she smiled to herself. The monk stopped and asked Rachel to leave her bicycle outside, as he showed her into a room.

"Father Savva will be with you shortly," said the monk, "Please wait here."

As Rachel waited, she reminded herself of what she was supposed to do. She had to hand over the letter to Savva Iliadis and no-one else. She knew that this person was the contact's alias and that he was certainly not a real member of the clergy.

A door opened and two monks came in. One of them introduced himself as the Abbot[66] of the monastery. He opened the side door which was located beneath an intricately ornate icon of the Virgin Mary and disappeared behind it. Rachel was left standing alone in the room with the other monk.

"Are you Savva Iliadis?" she asked.

The monk nodded.

"How can I be sure?"

The tall man pulled open his long monastic black frock and Rachel saw that he had two guns attached to his garment.

"I didn't mean to offend you," she said, "I was told to make sure that I spoke to Savva Iliadis and not an imposter."

Rachel reached inside her blouse and handed him the envelope which she had kept hidden on her for three days. After reading it, he looked up at her and said, "I'll see what I can do."

He left the room and did not return until sometime later. Rachel sat down on the floor to wait, giving in to exhaustion. The man returned and this time he was joined by a nun. She was told that females were not allowed to go beyond that point. Rachel followed the nun to an adjacent convent. She was taken up a flight of stairs to a kitchen where she was invited to sit down. The nun served her lentil soup with two thick slices of bread. Rachel hadn't eaten for a day and she gobbled the food down.

---

[66] A man who is the head of an abbey of monks.

When she had finished eating, the nun came and sat next to her. She told her that her name was Sister Sabina. She also told her that she was welcome to stay as long as she wanted at the convent. Rachel explained that she was in a hurry to get back to Salonica. Sister Sabina led Rachel to the guest room. Next to the room was a bathroom where the bath tub was filled with water.

"I just filled it up," said the nun, "The towel and soap are on the chair." Rachel removed her dirty clothes and placed them right outside the bathroom door, just as the nun had instructed her to. They were to be washed and dried by the sisters, ready for the next morning. Rachel immersed herself in the bath tub. The warm water soothed her cold and aching body. After her bath, Rachel found a nightgown and underwear laid out on the bed. She put them on and climbed into bed, snuggling under the covers.

The following morning Rachel awoke to a familiar smell drifting into her room. It was the same incense that was used in Father Nikolas' church, back in Salonica. It was Frankincense and myrrh resin that produced this sweet smell. Christina had once told Rachel about the incense. She looked around the room but felt very dizzy. She tried to stand up but fell back down onto the bed. The room was spinning. Rachel knew that she was not well. A few moments later Sister Sabina entered the room. She told Rachel that she had tried to wake her up a couple of hours before, but Rachel had mumbled something and carried on sleeping.

"You have a fever," said the nun.

She placed a wet cloth on Rachel's forehead.

"The only way to get rid of the flu is to sleep it off. Go back to sleep and soon I will bring you some chamomile tea."

Just as the nun had promised, she came back with tea but also with a thermometer. She helped Rachel to sit up in bed. She handed her the thermometer and told her to place it under her arm. Rachel removed the thermometer and handed it to the Sister.

"Your temperature is 40.2C," said the nun, "You'll need to rest for at least three days."

Rachel drank her tea and went back to sleep.

For the next three days Rachel was in and out of sleep, completely unaware of her surroundings. On the fourth morning, she opened her eyes and realised where she was. Sister Sabina immediately took Rachel's temperature. It had gone down to 38.5C. She brought Rachel some chicken soup and helped her to eat it.

The following morning Rachel felt strong enough to stand up. She was still very weak. It took another three days for Rachel to feel better. (That was the only time in her long life that she had been so sick)

Nine days after Rachel's arrival at the convent, she was completely healthy again.

Rachel was summoned back to the monastery which was just half a mile away. She was led into the same room that she had gone to upon her arrival. There she waited until Savva Iliadis came.

"I have good news for you," he said, "Father Nikolas' brother-in-law was released from the camp."

For a brief moment Rachel stared at him in disbelief before saying, "I can't believe it. I am so thrilled."

"You're a very brave young girl," he said.

He shook Rachel's hand and said, "We're always in need of new recruits."

"Thank you, that means a lot to me," replied Rachel, "I will definitely think it over."

The truth was that Rachel had no intention of joining any kind of resistance group. She only said she would consider it because she didn't want to offend Savva Iliadis.

That day was to be Rachel's last day in Serres. After lunch she went for a long walk around the grounds of the convent. She could smell the wonderful scents of spring in the air. She sat down on a log and as she gazed up at the hillside, Rachel's thoughts went to something completely unrelated to her current situation. As a high-school student, she really enjoyed the history of Ancient Greece and as she stared up at the dark green hills and gorgeous trees she couldn't help but wonder if this is what Mt. Olympus, the dwelling place of the Gods, must look like, because it was simply heaven.

Rachel spent her last evening with Sister Sabina. Their conversation made Rachel miss her mother terribly and that evening she prayed for her family's safe return to Salonica once the war was over.

In the early hours of the morning, Rachel was woken by one of the nuns. After breakfast, she was given a loaf of bread which she placed in her satchel. She hugged each nun leaving the longest hug for Sister Sabina. She mounted her bicycle and waved as she rode off.

The journey back to Salonica was much easier and less stressful. Most of the trip was downhill and very regularly she would pass signs that read 'SALONICA' with arrows pointing either right or left. Rachel hardly ever looked at her map, rather choosing to follow the signs. The three check points that she came across were without incident and once she had crossed into the county of Salonica, then there was nothing stopping her. That day she covered seventy kilometres and she arrived at Christina's door in around seven hours.

Rachel rang the doorbell. Moments later, Evangelia opened the front door. When she saw Rachel, she placed her hand on her mouth in surprise. Then she lifted her finger to her lips and silently said, "Shh," not wanting her untrustworthy neighbours to hear anything as Rachel went inside. The priest's wife, who had learnt of her brother's release, jumped up from her armchair and hugged Rachel tightly. They embraced for an entire minute. The rest of the family took turns in welcoming Rachel back. That evening Rachel slept at their apartment. They all stayed up very late as Rachel told in detail about her mission that had unexpectedly lasted nine long days.

CHAPTER EIGHT

Liberation

Rachel clearly remembers the day the Germans left Salonica. It was a Monday morning, the 30th of October 1944. It was about ten o'clock in the morning when she and Stella were in the sitting room looking through some French fashion magazines, that there was a knock on the door. It was Stella's neighbour. In an animated voice she told her that if she had a wireless she should turn it on. Apparently, the Germans are leaving the city and Salonica is free again." exclaimed the neighbour. Stella quickly ran into her husband's study and turned on the radio which they had been able to keep due to her husband's contacts[67].

Stella called Rachel to relay what was being said on the radio.

Rachel heard a male voice saying, "My fellow Greeks, the tyrannical enemy who brutally occupied us for the past three years have evacuated our sacred city and country. My fellow Greeks we are once again free." The Greek national anthem began to play. Rachel explained to Stella what was said. They hugged each other, tears streaming down their cheeks. They heard people shouting in the streets. They ran to their balcony and saw a mass of people cheering, waving Greek flags and shouting at the top of their lungs, "The Germans are gone, they're gone. Long live freedom."

---

[67] During the Nazi occupation of Greece, anyone in possession of a wireless had to turn it in. Anyone found with a wireless was primarily executed.

The joy of the people on the street was contagious. Stella and Rachel began waltzing around the apartment. The doorbell rang. It was Christina and Evangelia. They were both holding small Greek flags made out of paper. The four of them started hugging each other. They stood in a circle holding onto each other's shoulders. Evangelia began singing a Greek patriotic song and the four of them danced the hasaposerviko[68].

The celebratory mood was evident throughout the city and lasted for a few weeks. The sad reality was that as soon as the Germans left, a civil war broke out in Greece. In Salonica, Communist propaganda posters were put up all over the city. Soon, more posters appeared that reflected the right-wing political factions of Greece. Rachel mostly stayed indoors in order to avoid the skirmishes in downtown Salonica between the two rival groups. One Sunday afternoon in mid-October, Rachel and Christina were walking along the waterfront on Nikis Avenue when they came across an old acquaintance of Christina's family. There had been a lot of gossip about him for many years regarding his activities as a faithful member of the Communist Party of Greece.

"How are you Mr. Kosta?" asked Christina.

"How do you think I am?" he replied angrily, "I can't believe all this effort is going to go to waste."

"What do you mean?"

---

[68] A Greek folk dance which literally means 'fast butcher's dance'.

"I'll tell you exactly what I mean," he said as he smoked his cigarette, "That General Scobie[69] is a curse. There is no way that I'm going to allow his army to destroy everything that we've worked for."

Rachel and Christina looked at each other, for they were well aware that the British General, whom they supported, was in charge of suppressing the Communist Party in Greece.

"I wouldn't worry about it too much," said Christina, "At Church I will light a candle for you so that everything you wish for goes right."

He then stood up from the bench and for a moment he looked very angry. He then stepped forward and said in a very loud voice, "Did you say *right*?"

Rachel and Christina took a step back and were unable to speak. All Christina could do was nod.

"I'll be damned if things go right. From now on, everything will go left," he said as he motioned with his left arm.

"Yes, whatever you say," said Christina, "Greetings to your lovely wife." Both girls turned and hurried along. They didn't want to aggravate him any more.

The mood in Greece was very volatile. The situation remained tense until early 1945.[70]

---

[69] The British commander in Greece during the Greek civil war.
[70] There were a series of clashes fought in Athens from 3 December 1944 to 11 January 1945. The Greek left-wing resistance forces fought the British Army which was supported by the Greek Government.

Not much had changed for Rachel during the early months of 1945. On the 8th May the war officially ended. Stella's husband advised Rachel that she should try to reclaim her father's business. He suggested that she start the process while she waited for her family to return. The next day, Rachel and Stella went to the hacienda only to find that it had been completely destroyed. There were workers building a new building. Rachel approached one of the workers and told him that this was the site of her family home. He said that the city council has purchased the entire block and they were building on it.

Rachel was deeply disturbed by this information. The two women then went to her father's tin smith shop where a Greek Christian man had taken over the business. Rachel instantly recognised him as he had worked for her father. Her father had given him his machinery prior to being deported so that he could look after it until his return. The machinery was worth quite a lot. He told Rachel that he had bought the machinery from her father which she knew to be untrue.

Stella and her husband told Rachel that she should sue the former employee. They told her that she had a good chance of winning and that they would pay any court fees.

The summer of 1945 was spent talking to lawyers and making many court visits in order to obtain what was rightfully hers. The hardest thing was having to prove that the machinery was really her father's. After tracking down the man who had sold the machinery to her father in the early 1930's, Rachel was relieved when he agreed to testify in Rachel's favour.

"Your father was an honest and decent man," said the man to Rachel. Apparently her father had agreed to pay the machinery off in instalments. According to the seller, he was one of a few men to pay him back the full amount.

After a week in court, the Judge said that even though there was no evidence to prove whether or not Rachel's father had sold the machinery to his former employee, the Judge believed that the former employee was lying for he had changed his story a number of times and had been caught in his own lies during the trial.

The Judge had an expert appraise the machinery and he ordered the defendant to either give the machinery back to Rachel or pay it off in monthly instalments.

After the trial had ended, Rachel visited the man who had testified in her favour, in order to thank him. He told her that when her father returned, she must tell him to come and visit him. Rachel had no way of knowing at this stage, what had become of her father or the rest of her family.

The autumn of 1945 seemed to pass very slowly as Rachel waited to hear from or see her family again. Rachel and Stella would often go to the Jewish relief centre in downtown Salonica. Stella volunteered three times a week and on occasion Rachel would accompany her. She didn't particularly like to go because she felt depressed seeing the survivors who had returned from the Nazi death camps. They were skin and bone and there was a permanent sadness in their stare. One December afternoon, an emaciated man approached Rachel.

"Rachel Seror?" he asked.

"Yes," replied Rachel.

"Don't you recognise me?"

"You look familiar but I can't place you," said Rachel.

"I'm Victor," he said.

Rachel continued to stare at him in silence.

"I'm Alberto's son, your neighbour."

Rachel stood up and cried out, "Victor! Oh my God, I didn't recognise you."

They hugged each other tightly.

Rachel was annoyed with herself for not being able to recognise the boy next door whom she had grown up with. Victor and his family were seen as family by the Serors. Alberto was the accordion player who was at every function at the hacienda. That evening Victor was invited by Stella to stay at her house temporarily. He had gone to his house but, just like Rachel's, it had been knocked down. During his stay, Victor described the horror of the Auschwitz concentration camp. He had been lucky enough not to be gassed upon arrival but instead he was selected to work at the Monowitz-Buna[71] slave labour camp. He was the only one to survive from his entire family. As for Rachel's family, he never came across any of them during his time at Auschwitz.

A few weeks later on New Year's Eve, Rachel was at the Jewish relief centre again helping out when she noticed that two girls were staring at her from across the room. Rachel instantly knew that they were camp

---

[71] Also known as Auschwitz III, the Monowitz-Buna camp was one of the three main camps in the Auschwitz concentration camp system.

survivors because of their gaunt and haunted appearance. One of the girls' smiled at her. Rachel went up to them. They looked familiar but she was unable to remember their names.

"Aren't you Lola's sister?" asked one of the girls.

"Yes, I am" replied Rachel, "Have you seen my sister?"

"She was with us in the camp."

"Which camp?" asked Rachel.

"Both camps, Auschwitz and Ravensbruck."

"Is she alive?" she asked, her heart pounding in her chest.

"Yes, I believe she is."

"Is she here in Salonica?"

"No, she went to Belgium with other survivors."

Rachel hugged both girls at once before bursting into tears.

For the next hour or so, Rachel asked as many questions as she could but the girls didn't have all the answers. When Rachel asked them what they would do now that they were back, they said that they would be going to Palestine. They suggested that Rachel go with them. They exchanged addresses and made arrangements to meet up again. That evening as Rachel and Stella walked home, Rachel was saying how happy she felt knowing that her sister was alive and Stella reminded her that it was New Year's Eve and that St. Basil[72] had delivered her present one day early. After the New Year Holiday, Stella placed an inquiry at the Jewish relief centre on behalf of Rachel. The inquiry was through the International Red

---

[72] In the Orthodox Christian culture, St. Basil is Santa Clause and the presents are delivered on New Year's Day.

Cross which passed the information on to the Belgian Red Cross. It was a request for confirmation that Lola Seror was living in Belgium. All Rachel could do now was wait. A month later, Rachel's happiness was shattered when she bumped into an old acquaintance at the Jewish relief centre. His name was Jacko and he was her father's very good friend. He owned a coffee shop at Bexinari[73] which he had once again opened upon his return from Auschwitz. As soon as Rachel saw him she hugged him and became very excited and hopeful that her father was alive too.

"What news do you have?" she asked.

Jacko looked at her and placed his hand on her shoulder.

"I'm sorry Rachel, but your father did not survive."

Rachel sat down. Her whole body trembled.

"What happened?" she asked.

"Why don't you come by the coffee shop tomorrow and I will tell you all about it."

The following morning Rachel had second thoughts about going to visit Jacko. In a way she didn't want to know what happened to her father. The knowledge that he was dead was traumatic enough for her. Stella insisted on Rachel going and she offered to accompany her. When they arrived they sat at one of the tables and the waiter brought them a glass of water and Turkish coffee. When Jacko was finally free, he came and sat at their table and told them all about his horrific experience. He said that Auschwitz was nothing more than hell on earth. Jacko said that they had no solid food - just some soup with the occasional turnip and potato in it.

---

[73] A small area in the district of Salonica.

They were given a slice of stale bread which tasted like sawdust and a cup of ersatz[74] coffee in the morning. They were beaten, screamed at and constantly degraded. But despite all this Jacko thought he had it good because at least he didn't have to empty the latrines. He explained that this job was given to Rachel's father. Whenever the latrines were full they would have to scoop the faeces out with a shovel into a bucket and then go and empty the bucket. They did the same thing over until the latrines were empty. With no gloves and no face masks, those who did this job had constant intestinal problems. The average life span for these men was three months. Rachel's father lived for six months which showed how strong he was. Rachel was extremely distressed when Jacko told her about her father's final days. For at least one week, Rachel's father had diarrhoea. One afternoon he developed acute stomach pain and fell to the ground inside the barrack. He lay there crying out in pain until he died. His body lay on the ground for three more days until the kapo[75] ordered some of the men to take his body outside.

"He was left there all alone face down in his vomit," said Jacko.

"But why didn't anyone help him?" asked Rachel.

"He had dysentery. We were all afraid of catching it."

The tragic news of Rachel's father's death sent her into a downward spiral of despair. For the next two months she sat in Stella's apartment, alone

---

[74] A substitute coffee made from acorns and was a much poorer quality than real coffee.
[75] Nazi concentration camp prisoners who were given privileges in return for supervising forced labour.

with her own thoughts. However, this emotional setback was not to last for too long. In May of 1946, Rachel received a telegram from the Belgian Red Cross confirming the news that her sister Lola was alive. This news was so unbelievable for her that she kept the telegram in her pocket for many months. Stella got word through the Jewish relief agency that Lola had also been notified that Rachel was alive and that Rachel would soon receive a letter from her sister.

Rachel anxiously waited for the postman's daily delivery. One morning her prayers were answered when, in Stella's mailbox, there was a letter from Belgium addressed to Rachel Seror.

Rachel's hand trembled as she opened the letter. She instantly recognised the handwriting as Lola's. As she read, tears of joy streamed down her face. She now had valid proof that her beloved sister was truly alive. She was shocked to discover that her sister was living in Brussels with a Belgian-Jewish couple and was engaged to Morry who was the couple's nephew. Morry was a Polish Jew who had survived multiple death camps. The letter continued with a request. Lola was without any identity papers and she needed Rachel to obtain her birth certificate and send it over to Brussels immediately as Lola and Morry wanted to get married.

For Rachel, this news was a double-edged sword. On one hand she was so thrilled that her sister was alive, and for the first time in three years she knew that she wasn't all alone anymore. On the other hand, she felt empty inside as she had no idea how long it would take for her to see her sister again. Lola had made it clear in the letter that she wasn't going to go back to Salonica. She explained that after their marriage, her husband would sail to Australia as he had some distant cousins there. He would then sponsor Lola and bring her to Australia.

Rachel was devastated to think about Lola being so far away and had no idea when she would see her again. She managed to put all those feelings aside and concentrated on the present. She had a request from her beloved sister and she had every intention of fulfilling it.

The following morning Rachel and Stella made their way to the Registry of Births, Deaths and Marriages in downtown Salonica. Initially they were told it would take up to an hour to process the document but they ended up staying there the entire day. All the documents had been burnt in a fire during the war. Rachel was told not to be discouraged because they could create a new birth certificate for her sister. Rachel didn't know what to make of all this but it didn't matter because she was grateful that she wouldn't be leaving without a birth certificate. After a long day of waiting, the birth certificate was ready. On their way home Rachel and Stella stopped at the General Post Office in Salonica. They did not waste any time in sending Lola her brand new birth certificate.

The entire summer of 1946 was to be an emotional upheaval for Rachel. She received letters from her sister in Belgium saying that once she goes to Australia she will send for Rachel. She was given strict instructions not to go anywhere. Many of Rachel's friends who had returned from the camps told her that there was a boat leaving for Palestine every three weeks. Rachel was encouraged to go with them. The truth was that deep down Rachel desperately wanted to go to her ancestral homeland but she was reluctant to leave in case anyone from her family was still alive and would return to Salonica. She wanted to be there if they returned. She was also torn about leaving because of Lola's insistence that she not go anywhere. For three months she was going back and forth in her mind about what she should do. In late August when another boat was ready to set sail, her closest friends departed for Palestine. Rachel decided to go with them. At the time, the entry of Jewish refugees into Palestine was illegal so Rachel knew that she was to embark on something that might not work out but she had decided to give it a go. On the night before she was scheduled to leave, Rachel dreamt of her brother Moishe. He gave her a bunch of white flowers in the dream. As soon as she woke up she knew that she could not go to Palestine. That morning she discussed her decision with Stella. She resolved to put aside her dream of going to Palestine. It was just not the right time.

CHAPTER NINE

New Beginnings

In September 1946, Christina came to visit Rachel with the news that her family would be leaving Thessaloniki. Her father was being transferred to the island of Lemnos where one of the smaller chapels had recently lost their parish priest due to illness. Christina gave Rachel her new address and made her promise to visit them in Lemnos as soon as possible. They sat talking for hours that day - reminiscing about the past three years which had been extraordinarily eventful for both of them. Rachel confided to Christina that she had been looking for work. Apart from anything else, Rachel wanted to pay board and lodging to Stella as she had been living in her house for two and a half years without having given her a cent. Christina told her that there were a few jobs available at the British Army recreational centre that was located on the outskirts of town.
"I'm sure you will find a job there," said Christina.
She hugged Rachel and Stella as she bid them farewell. As the elevator doors were closing, Rachel waved to her dear friend for one last time. Rachel had no way of knowing at the time, that she would never see Christina again.
The following morning Rachel got up early and made her way to the British Army centre across town. As she did not speak English, a Greek man who worked there was the interpreter during her brief job interview. At the end of the interview she was surprised to find out that she was

hired. She was told that she was now an employee of NAAFI.[76] Rachel agreed to start immediately. She was taken to the canteen and shown how to make sandwiches, teacakes and scones. One of her jobs was to serve at the counter where she handed out cups of tea and food to the soldiers. This job was Rachel's introduction to the English language and it wasn't too long before she spoke fluently.

Rachel worked at the Centre from Monday to Saturday. When she received her first pay cheque, she was totally elated. Stella refused to accept her money so Rachel made Friday evenings a ritual. She would go to the shops and buy small gifts for Stella and her daughters.

Rachel was lucky enough to have a lift home every day. One of the soldiers who worked at the canteen had a Jeep and he dropped her off at home every evening, except on Fridays when she was dropped off in the city centre.

During her first week at work, Rachel was told that the manager of the canteen was on leave. He had gone to visit his family in England and he was due to return at the end of the month. Soon enough, the month passed and Corporal George Curtis, the canteen manager, came back. As soon as he laid eyes on Rachel, it was love at first sight for him. For Rachel it would take a little bit longer to fall in love.

"Hi there, I'm George Curtis," said a tall handsome stranger.

"Hello," said Rachel, "My name is Maria Seror."

---

[76] The **Navy, Army and Air Force Institutes (NAAFI)** is an organisation created by the British government in 1921 to run the catering and recreational establishments needed by the armed forces.

(When the war ended Rachel had decided to keep her new Christian name because that's how she had become known to most of her new acquaintances.)

On his first day back at work the manager told Rachel that he would be taking her home every evening. As the weeks went by, George began dating Rachel. They went to the movies, to an amusement park and for long walks along Salonica's promenade. One morning at work, a soldier approached Rachel and asked her out. She was silent as George interjected, "She's my girlfriend," he said.

"Yeah but she's not your fiancée," said the soldier.

"She will be soon, so lay off," said George.

Then that evening when he dropped her off at Stella's house, he came inside. They sat in the living room and he told her that he didn't want her to work anymore. He said that he would pay her the wages from his own pocket. He took out a small box and opened it. There was a sparkling ring in the box.

"Maria, I want you to be my wife," said the British Corporal.

"Yes," said Rachel. She was not able to say anything else because in the excitement of the moment, she had forgotten all of the English that she had learnt during the past two months.

George's proposal was in November 1946 and they set their wedding date for 24th of March 1947. George's friends at NAAFI threw an engagement party for the happy couple. The canteen where the soldiers ate had been decorated with balloons and streamers. There was a huge sign against the wall saying,

CONGRATULATIONS ON YOUR ENGAGEMENT
MARIA AND GEORGE

There were plenty of sandwiches, teacakes and an abundance of alcohol which some of the soldiers had managed to sneak in even though no alcohol was allowed on the premises. According to George, every time there was a wedding or an engagement party, those in charge turned a blind eye to the alcohol. Rachel could not have been happier. She immediately wrote a letter to her sister Lola in Belgium asking her to come to the wedding. Unfortunately, Lola was unable to attend as she was waiting for her husband to send her a visa from Australia.

For the next four months, Stella helped Rachel with all the preparations. She even hired Rachel's wedding dress for her. A few weeks before the wedding, Stella told Rachel and George that she was going to buy the wedding cake for them as she was hosting a reception at her house after the nuptials. She generously invited all of George's friends which she came to regret when her huge house was overflowing with people on the day.

On the morning of the 24th of March 1947, Rachel awoke with mixed emotions. She expected to be totally elated that day but instead it was a bittersweet feeling that she experienced. On one hand she was very excited and couldn't believe it was her wedding day but on the other hand, not one member of her family was present to share this wonderful day with her. Rachel put the heartache aside and told herself that she wouldn't allow her negative thoughts to ruin the moment. Stella and her husband drove Rachel to the British registry office and Stella's husband, the Italian

Baron, gave her away. After the brief civil ceremony and the exchanging of wedding rings, they all made their way to a photographic studio where many photos were taken. After that, they went back to Stella's house where the caterers had already set up everything. They cut the wedding cake, took more photos and then Rachel and George had their first dance as the gramophone played in the background and the wedding guests stood around watching.

Around half past seven in the evening the British soldiers began arriving, some of them with their 'dames'[77]. By eight o'clock there were at least forty people in Stella's house. Some were drinking and others were dancing to swing music. The soldiers had brought along their own alcohol and their American records. Stella and the Baron kept looking at each other but they considered it rude to ask them to leave. Rachel could see that this was an unwanted intrusion but she was so happy that she didn't allow it to bother her. The entire evening Rachel and George were in each other's arms, talking to guests or just standing there with permanent smiles on their faces.

Rachel and George spent their wedding night in one of the guest rooms at Stella's house and the next day Rachel moved into George's flat.

Three months later, the newlyweds were thrilled to learn that George was being promoted from Corporal to Sergeant. The blissful happiness wasn't to last long as George became more and more homesick. He wanted to take his bride to England to start a brand new life together. The problem

---

[77] An American slang word for women which comes from the word *damsel*.

was that Rachel wanted to remain in Salonica as she still secretly hoped that some of her family members would somehow return home.

Eventually, Rachel succumbed to her husband's persuasion and agreed to leave.

Two nights before their departure, Rachel visited Stella for one last time. Rachel confided in Stella that she did not want to go to England as she didn't feel confident enough in the English language. She was still conversing in Italian with her husband. She also felt that if she had to go to a foreign country, she would prefer to go to Australia to be with her sister, Lola. Stella comforted her and advised her to go to England with her husband. She suggested that from there they could immigrate to Australia in due course.

On the morning of Rachel and George's departure, they met Stella and the Baron at the port. Their goodbyes to each other were extremely emotional. Rachel was very sad to leave her birthplace. She was also devastated at having to say goodbye to Stella who was like a sister to her.

Their journey to England was uneventful. They sailed for ten days and the ship made some stops along the way. On a cold October morning in 1947 the ship docked at Portsmouth, England where Rachel and George were to begin their new life. When they disembarked from the ship, George's parents and sister were there waiting for them. Rachel felt a bit distant and strange. She knew that it would take time to warm up to them and her new environment.

Portsmouth is a port city in Hampton County and is situated on Portsea Island. It was George's hometown where his family had lived for many generations. Over the next few months, George gave Rachel a guided tour of his birthplace making sure to cover every nook and cranny. Almost immediately, Rachel's spoken English began to improve and six months later she began to converse permanently in English with her husband. George resumed the work he did before the war. He worked with his father who was a blacksmith, a profession that had been passed down from father to son over the centuries. The Curtis family bought and sold horses and they made metal horseshoes with the latest machinery. They were the only ones in all of Portsmouth who owned top, state of the art sharpening equipment. Their small business thrived as the townspeople brought all of their knives and tools to them to be sharpened.

A specific component of the equipment, which was created by George's father, was seen as so unique that it was later exhibited in a museum.

The next few years seemed to pass quite slowly for Rachel. She spent a lot of time at home with George's mother and sister. On Sunday's she always accompanied George and his family to church, despite not being a Christian, for she saw it as her wifely duty. Most days she kept her distance and spent a lot of time sitting in her room alone. There wasn't anything apart from her dear husband that she really liked. Rachel found it very difficult to adjust to the climate. The cold rainy weather was constantly making her sick. Even the summer months were not very warm.

"This is not Greece," George constantly reminded her, "It's England and it's never as warm as Greece."

"Can't we go to Australia?" Rachel asked her husband, "My sister writes how beautiful the weather is all year round."

Lola wrote long letters and she always had something positive to say about Australia. The summers were hot and the temperature during the winter months was very much like Salonica's winter. There were plenty of jobs available and housing was affordable as was food and other household items. She wrote that they ate meat every second day. Rachel thought that Australia must be a wealthy country because back home in Salonica, despite being from a middle-class family, they had meat once every fortnight and when the war came they were lucky to even taste it. Despite Rachel's pleas, George wanted to give England a go before moving to another country. Rachel became deeply depressed and cried nearly every day. George's mother felt sorry for her and one day she sat George down and told him to take Rachel to Australia because she was extremely miserable in England.

George agreed to go to Australia with his wife when he learnt of the 'Assisted Passage Migration Scheme' which had been created by the Australian Government in 1945. All adult British subjects were charged only ten pounds for the fare. And so Rachel and George set sail as ten-pound poms[78] on the 6th of February, 1952 – the same day that King George VI passed away.

Six and a half weeks later, on the 24th of March while still on the ship, Rachel and George celebrated their fifth wedding anniversary. Rachel surprised George with a gold lighter that she had purchased in England. On the 30th of March, Rachel and George arrived in Port Melbourne, Australia. It took a few hours to clear customs on board the ship. Eventually, Rachel and George were ready to disembark. As they descended the stairs, all Rachel could see was a sea of people looking anxiously up at the ship trying to spot their loved ones. Lola had told Rachel in a letter that she would be waiting for her at the port. As Rachel scanned the crowd she began to feel nervous, not knowing if she would be able to recognise her baby sister after nine long and difficult years apart. As Rachel and George struggled through the crowd they heard a voice shouting out in Greek, "Rahill, Rahill[79]."

Just ahead of her, Rachel spotted her beautiful sister who was now all grown up. Lola was waving excitedly at them. Rachel noticed that her sister was visibly pregnant. Next to Lola was her husband Morris, holding their fourteen month old daughter, Greta.

Rachel approached Lola, calmly placed her bags on the ground and then threw herself in her sister's arms. Their embrace lasted for a long time as both sisters were sobbing, not wanting to let go. They introduced their

---

[78] 'Ten Pound Poms' is a colloquial term used in Australia and New Zealand to describe British subjects who migrated to those countries after the Second World War.
[79] The Greek word for Rachel.

husbands to each other and Rachel kissed baby Greta. They all piled into Morris's car and a short time later they arrived at Lola's house in Richmond. The house was at the front of their bakery. Lola's husband, a Polish-Jewish Holocaust survivor, had opened the bakery in 1947. He knew the bakery business well as his own father had owned a bakery back in Poland before the war. Rachel and George were given the largest room. They stayed there for quite a while until they were able to stand on their own two feet. For the first few months Rachel and Lola spent every hour of every day together. They had so much to catch up on. Lola, a survivor of Auschwitz told her sister that when their cousin arrived at the camp she told Lola that Rachel had escaped from the ghetto. It was that knowledge that had kept Lola going as she struggled to stay alive every day that she was in that hell. Rachel told Lola of her experiences in the many hiding places.

There was one thing that Lola found hard to get used to and that was that Rachel now had a new name. Rachel's husband called her Maria and her passport read Maria Curtis with no middle name. Rachel explained to Lola how Maria was her name when she was in hiding and after the war she chose to keep it. Eventually, Lola got used to calling her Maria.

One thing that both sisters could never get used to was the fact that not a single member of their family in Salonica survived. In the coming years there would be many moments when Rachel and Lola would mourn together the loss of their loved ones. They held fast to their belief that one day, in another life, they would all be together again.

Family Photos

It is very rare for Holocaust Survivors to have family photographs from before the war.

These precious pre-war photos and photos taken during the war were hidden by Maria.

Salonica 1937 – Maria

Salonica 1938 – Israel Seror

(Father of Maria and Lola)

Salonica 1939 – Second from right is Moishe Seror (older brother to Maria and Lola) and front right is their cousin

Salonica 1939 - Maria on holiday

Salonica 1940 - Maria (left) and Lola (right)

Salonica, early 1940's – Purim party with friends –

Bottom left - Maria dressed as Chico Marx

Salonica, early 1940's – Maria dressed as Chico Marx for a Purim party

Salonica circa 1941 – Maria's friend Stella and her daughters

Salonica 1942 – Lola (left) and Maria (right)

Greece circa 1944 Maria (left) and a friend she met while living under a false identity

Salonica 1945 after the Germans had left Greece.
The Greek Orthodox priest – Centre – was a good friend of the Russian priest, Father Nikolas, who hid Maria

Salonica 1945 - Maria after liberation

Salonica 1946 – Maria – second row far right. Some of these friends were survivors of Auschwitz. The man in the second row far left survived Auschwitz and was able to give Maria information about her father and brother and how they died in Auschwitz.

Salonica circa late 1946 – Maria and her beau, George Curtis

Belgium 1946 - Lola

Salonica 1947 – Maria and George wedding day. Maria's friend Stella and her husband (back Left). Stella's two daughters are the bridesmaids.

Salonica 1947 - Maria passport photo

Salonica 1948 – Maria and George Curtis

Melbourne Early 1950's – Far right – Maria; Second from Right – Maria's husband George, with friends at a night club

Melbourne 1952 – Maria (left) and Lola (right) at a dance

Melbourne 1954 - Maria and her daughter Margaret

(approximately eight months old)

Melbourne 1960 - Maria in a beautiful dress that Lola bought for her

Surfer's Paradise 1966 – far right – Lola; 2nd from Right – Morris; Far left – Harry Putt; Second from left – Maria

Melbourne 2017 - Maria and Lola at an exhibition about the Jews of Greece at the Melbourne Jewish Museum

(Photo: Carol Gordon)

Melbourne 2018 - Maria

(Photo: Tiah Gordon)

Melbourne 2018 – Lola

(Photo: Tiah Gordon)

Melbourne 2018 - Maria and Lola

(Photo: Tiah Gordon)

BOOK TWO

LOLA'S STORY

Chapter One

A Life of Dreams and Change

Salonica, Greece

There was much joy and celebration in the Seror house on the 16th of May, 1926 as baby Lola was welcomed into the world. Moishe and Rachel were very excited to have a baby sister to dote on. Lola was a happy baby who loved the attention. From a young age, Lola was vivacious and creative. A dreamer with a vivid imagination. She couldn't wait to start school and thrived in the stimulation of that environment.

Barely eight years of age, Lola would sneak into her parents' bedroom, and dress up in her mother's high-heeled shoes and long evening gowns, adorning herself with a matching necklace. She would put on red lipstick and play Sophia Vebo's record on the gramophone. She would then sing and dance for hours on end in front of her mother's full length mirror. "Our daughter is going to become a film star one day," Lola's mother would often be heard saying to her husband.

Lola's father was a tall sturdy man who had his own tin-making business, which was much in demand as tinned food conserves were beginning to be marketed in Greece. He worked long hours trying to provide for his ever growing family.

Salonica, Greece
March 25, 1940

It was early spring and the weather was glorious. Not a cloud in the sky and the sun was warm enough to fill up one's soul.
"Lola, Lola," yelled Katerina. Ahead in the crowd, Lola could see her best friend waving to her. It was Greek Independence Day and every school in Salonica had gathered in the main city square to take part in the annual parade. Every student was dressed in blue and white. The girls wore a blue skirt and white top and the boys in blue pants and white shirts. Small Greek paper flags were everywhere. As Lola made her way towards Katerina, pushing eagerly through the crowd, she saw her big brother Moishe with his friends smiling at her. When she reached her best friend they embraced warmly. They admired each other's blue and white hair bows which they had purchased a few days earlier. As they chatted away excitedly, the whistle was blown for the students to get into three columns from the oldest to the youngest. All the students in perfect formation began to march, their feet bopping up and down, their arms swinging back and forth and the teachers marching beside them could be heard saying, "One two, one two," as they made their way, soldier-like, along Venizelou Avenue.
As they passed the crowd that had gathered at the edge of the sidewalk, Lola as usual looked out for her grandmother Joya Capon who, every year, was seated in a chair that she brought with her, waiting proudly to see her grandchildren march by.

They passed by all the dignitaries and gathered on the side of the square. When the speeches were done, the entire crowd stood to attention as the flag was raised and the Philharmonic Orchestra played the Greek National Anthem.

Once everyone dispersed, Lola's brother and sister found her and they went to meet up with their parents and grandmother Joya. They all went home to a beautifully set table and a celebratory lunch that their mother had prepared. They spoke excitedly, sharing accounts of the day's events. Once they had finished their meal, Lola made her way to the front of the house where her friends had gathered. They played their favourite skipping game. Carefree and full of joy, these were the most beautiful days in Lola's life.

That summer of 1940 was not only to be a most memorable one but also the very last one they were to have as free citizens. They spent it, as they did every year, at the Chalcidice Peninsula. Only an hour and a half from Salonica, the family would travel there by train. They would spend all of July and August on the Kassandra coast in their summer bungalow which Lola's great-grandfather had built seventy-five years earlier. With its crystal clear waters and sun-drenched shoreline, this was the Seror family's second home. Every day was the same routine. They would spend the day at the beach swimming, sunbathing and building sand castles. After a hearty lunch, the entire family would lie down for their afternoon siesta on the blankets that mother had placed under the pine trees, whose branches formed natural umbrellas. The siesta was a family tradition which Lola's Sephardic ancestors had brought with them from Spain four hundred years earlier. The tragic story of the expulsion of the Sephardic Jews from the Iberian Peninsula had been passed down from generation to generation.

"We Jews lived in peace side by side with our Muslim and Christian neighbours," said grandma Joya to her grandchildren.

"Why did you leave?" asked Lola.

"I did not leave. Our forefathers were forced to flee four hundred years ago."

"But why?"

"Why?" responded grandma Joya. "I will tell you why. Because they were not willing to convert to Christianity. That is why they came to beautiful Salonica, where we have practiced our religion freely ever since."

These stories were told to the children as soon as they were old enough to understand. They were aware of their ancestors' perils but that was all in the past. Nothing could have prepared them for what was still to come.

Until 1940, the Seror family had three children. Moishe the oldest and the only boy was eighteen years old, followed by Rachel who was sixteen years old and the youngest being Lola who was fourteen. Being the youngest child she was spoilt and she remembers being her father's favourite, often accompanying him to the Synagogue on Saturday mornings. She could not wait for the Sinagoga[80] service to finish for her

---

[80] *Spanish/Ladino* A Jewish Synagogue

father would buy her a kosher[81] koulouri[82] coated with sesame seeds, which she devoured by the time they got home.

Summer turned into autumn and life was floating by as usual. Two events took place at that time that changed Lola's family. Coincidentally, they both fell on exactly the same day, Monday, the 28th of October. At two o'clock in the morning, Lola was awoken by a crying baby. She got out of bed and ran to her mother's room. There in her mother's arms lay the tiniest baby girl.

"This is Mathilde your sister," said mother.

Lola sat beside her and gazed at the baby who by this stage had stopped crying. She was so thrilled to see that she had a younger sister.

"Now I have two sisters," said Lola.

"Yes, you do," said mother.

Lola then moved to the side as the midwife leaned forward to pick up the baby.

Lola's gaze followed her as she placed the baby gently into the brand new crib that her grandmother had bought. Moishe and Rachel were also standing by the crib, admiring their new-born sibling.

"You're not the baby of the family anymore, Lola" said Moishe.

Lola smiled as she nodded and shrugged her shoulders.

"Alright," said father, "Everyone off to bed, you have school tomorrow."

---

[81] *Hebrew* Food that is fit for consumption, according to Jewish law
[82] *Greek* A ring shaped bread roll

Moishe, Rachel and Lola left their parents' bedroom and quietly made their way back to their beds, which unbeknownst to them was to be their last night as free citizens of Greece.

Later that morning, just before going to school, Lola went into her mother's bedroom to look at the baby. She looked so angelic lying there.
"Lola," said mother softly, "Come here."
Lola approached the bed and sat right beside her mother.
"Are you excited?" asked Mother.
"Yes," replied Lola. "I can't believe I have a baby sister. She looks so adorable."
"Let me give you a kiss," said mother.
Lola leaned over and hugged her mother tightly.
"El Dios[83] mazi sou[84]," said mother as she kissed her daughter on the forehead.
Lola left and was so excited that she couldn't get to school fast enough to tell her friends the wonderful news. The school bell rang and Lola and her friends lined up in the school yard for assembly.
This morning however was different in that the teachers were nowhere to be seen. The students waited in silence. Ten minutes later all the teachers came slowly, one by one, out of the school building. The school principal made her way to the podium to make an announcement.
"Good morning ladies," she said as her voice cracked.

---

[83] *Spanish/Ladino* God
[84] *Greek* With you

"Good morning Madam Principal," echoed the three hundred female voices that had assembled on the school yard.

"This morning it was announced on the radio that our Prime Minister Mr. Metaxas has responded to the Italian Ambassador's ultimatum. Our Government was told to allow the Italian Army to occupy freely. If their answer is 'No' then there would be a forced invasion. For those of you who haven't yet heard, the Prime Minister's answer was "OXI[85]."
Suddenly there was a thunderous applause and for the first time the students were not told to stop. Instead, the clapping continued for at least a minute longer.

"As of three hours ago, the enemy is attacking our frontier on the Greek-Albanian border. It is with great sorrow that I announce to you that our country is at war with Italy."

This time there was no clapping. Instead an eerie silence fell upon the school yard on that chilly autumn day.

"Therefore, as of now until further notice," continued the principal, "You are excused from attending school."

The Greek flag was raised and the National Anthem was sung by the entire school. The students then dispersed. Lola felt a hand on her shoulder. It was her sister Rachel.

"Come on, let's go home," said Rachel.

For the next three days, the mood in the Seror home was relaxed as everyone went about their business and took turns to cuddle the new born baby. On the Friday morning, just before midday, they heard a very loud

---

[85] *Greek* **No**

explosion. Lola was in the kitchen with her mother helping her prepare for the Sabbath. The china bowl that she was holding fell to the floor. The sound of the bowl shattering into many pieces was not even heard above the deafening sound of the enemy's bombs.

"Lola," shouted mother, "Go quickly! Hide behind the couch."

Mother hurried to the bedroom and took the baby into her arms. She went back downstairs and joined Lola. The Italian Air Force was relentless. The bombs were falling in quick succession. Mother was calling to the other children.

"Rachel, Moishe, Rachel, Moishe."

But there was no reply.

After what seemed like a very long time, the bombing stopped. There was complete silence followed by the sound of the ambulance sirens.

Mother stood up, still clutching the baby.

"Lola," she said.

"Yes mama."

"Stay here until I tell you it's safe to move."

She made her way slowly around the house.

"Thank God," she muttered under her breath.

The house had been spared from any bombing. She went back into her bedroom and placed the baby in the crib. As she turned, Lola was standing there.

"Didn't I tell you not to move?"

"I have to find Moishe and Rachel… and baba," she said.

"Your father's at his workshop, hopefully he's alright."

They made their way down to the kitchen and out to the front of the house. In the distance, they saw Moishe running towards them with baba behind him. They were all relieved to see each other. Within ten minutes, Rachel had also arrived. She was at her friend's house when the bombing began. The family had miraculously survived the bombing raid and in their prayers on that Friday night during Kiddush[86] , they gave thanks to the Almighty.

---

[86] *Hebrew* The Jewish prayer recited over a cup of wine in the home ushering in the Sabbath (on a Friday night)

Chapter Two

The Lull

Salonica, Greece

The winter of 1940-1941 was very harsh. It was much colder than it had been in previous years. But the cold seemed trivial when one thought of the Greek soldiers fighting on the Albanian front, in five feet of snow. It was a time of constant news reports blaring from the radio. The Greek army had a number of victories, pushing the Italians all the way back into Albania. The pride and morale of the Greek people was at an all-time high.

After the evening meal, Lola's father would read excerpts to his family from the daily newspaper.

"Can you believe it?"

"Believe what baba," replied Lola.

"Mussolini's army is the entire population of our country. And we managed to defeat them."

"I hope Beni comes back alive. My cousin doesn't need another tragedy," interrupted mother.

Benjamin was the youngest child of aunt Violetta. Out of her eight children, she was now left with only three. One of the children was stillborn, two had died from illness and the other two had met an untimely death when their boat overturned one summer at the Thermaic Gulf just off the coast of Kalamaria.

Beni had volunteered for the army in November of 1940 when Greece had been drawn into the war.

"He'll be alright," said Moishe. "I don't know anyone stronger or more courageous than Beni."

Aunt Violetta's youngest son ended up surviving the battles that raged on the Albanian front, only to be transported two years later, to Auschwitz-Birkenau, where he was a Sonderkommando[87] for eleven months before being executed.

By early spring, most Greeks, including Lola, believed that the brief war had come to an end. Influenced by all the reports that she had heard on the wireless during the winter, she was convinced that it was all over.

"We won!" she cried out excitedly, "My teacher told us that we pushed the Italians all the way back to Rome."

"But what about the Germans?" asked Moishe.

"What about them?" replied Lola's older sister.

"We can't exactly ignore them. Certain news reports are implying that the Germans will come to their ally's defence."

"Well let's hope that that never happens," said father.

---

[87] Jewish prisoners who were forced on threat of their own deaths, to aid with the disposal of gas chamber victims during the Holocaust.

A few weeks later, the unthinkable occurred. The Germans marched into Salonica after a long and hard fought battle with the Greek army. The streets were completely empty and the enemy soldiers marched to the German military band that was playing war tunes.

"Mama," cried Lola as she entered the house, "The Germans are here, I saw them marching down Nikis Avenue."

Before mother had time to reply, father rushed into the house.

"Where are the children?" he cried.

"They're all here, except for Moishe," replied mother.

"The Germans are here, they've just entered Salonica," he said.

"I saw them," exclaimed Lola, "There was a band playing beautiful music."

Lola's parents looked at each other.

"Well at least they didn't bomb us like the Italians did," he said.

"Let's hope," said mother, "That they stay for a very short time, because if they don't, only God knows what the future holds."

By the end of spring, Lola had forgotten about the war around her. Nothing had changed for her. She continued going to school and everything seemed as normal as it was before the invaders had entered their city. It wasn't until the summer of 1941 that Lola began to feel a little uneasy. For the first time ever, the Seror family did not go to the Chalcidice peninsula. Instead, they stayed home and had to host her father's cousins who came from Thrace after leaving in the middle of the night with just their clothes on their backs. Germany put Bulgaria in control of north-eastern Greece and the persecution of the Jewish communities had begun. Lola had to get used to having people living in their house, even though she was very fond of Uncle Ari and his family.

"Thank you for putting us up," said uncle Ari, "Word spread at home that the Germans were allowing the Jews to live in peace in Salonica."

"Not exactly," said father. "They've taken over our hospitals, they've plundered most of our Synagogues and they have made quite a few arrests. Let us hope that it doesn't get any worse."

Lola's family had so far been lucky enough not to be affected by the Nazis as others were. Their refugee relatives remained with them until October when their father managed to find a small apartment for them.

The autumn months passed quickly. Before Lola knew it, it was already December. One afternoon, prior to the Christmas holidays, Lola noticed how her mother had put on weight. It made an impression on her because the food for the family was becoming scarce. Most of their food was now being grown in the vegetable patch which her parents had at the back of the house.

"Rachel, come here," said Lola, "Have you noticed how mum has put on weight."

"She's put on weight because she's pregnant," said her older sister.

"Pregnant?" sighed Lola, "Not again."

"Get ready for another sister or brother."

"Oh my gosh."

"Remember what grandma Joya always says to us?"

Lola shook her head.

"Every baby that comes into the world is of God."

"You're right," said Lola, "She does say that."

Lola retreated to her bedroom to process the news. She was a naive fifteen year old girl who was still trying to grasp the ways of the world. She went back down to the kitchen to take another curious look at her mother's tummy.

Just two short months later, in February of 1942, the newest addition to the Seror family was born. She was named Arietta, a common Judeo-Spanish name which had been carried down from one generation to the next.

Lola Seror's family now seemed complete.

"Let us praise the Lord," said father during the evening meal. "He has given me one boy and four beautiful girls. What else can a man ask for?"

At this point life seemed content, just rolling by despite the hardships of the occupation.

"Let us hope that this war ends soon."

"Yes, let us hope," said mother.

The unusual lull that the Jewish community of Salonica was experiencing, began to fade slowly. In the summer of 1942 an incident occurred that disturbed Lola. One afternoon in mid-June she and her brother Moishe were visiting their mother's uncle. They were sitting in the courtyard under the falling fig leaves, drinking orange juice, when they heard the sound of a motor car approaching. The car stopped outside the house and they heard car doors slamming, followed by the ringing of the neighbour's door bell. They all sat there in silence, not knowing what to expect. They heard some kind of commotion coming from next door. A woman was wailing as the unexpected visitors left the house. As soon as the noise of the motor car faded into the distance, their uncle jumped up to investigate what was happening next door. The children stayed in the house, terrified. The uncle hurried back in with the news that the Germans had taken away their neighbour. He was suspected of being a member of the resistance. That night Lola wasn't able to sleep. She could hear her parents talking.

"He was arrested because he's Jewish," said her father, "I know Haim Bibas. He would never get involved with anything that would put him and his family in jeopardy."

"You think you know him," whispered her mother.

"I'm telling you," said her father, "It's because he's Jewish. Let us pray that the Germans don't arrest me."

"Don't even think that, let alone say it out loud," said Lola's mother.

Over the next few weeks, Lola tried very hard to put that incident behind her and just when she had started to, another horrific episode took place, this time involving her family members. In early July 1942, the Germans posted a banner compelling all Jewish males aged between 18 and 45 to assemble at Liberty Square. This of course included Lola's father who was 44 years of age and her only brother who had just turned 19.

"Don't go," said mother. "I have a bad feeling about this, they will take you away and we'll never see you again."

Mother's instincts were hardly ever wrong. But father was also suspicious and he spent the next few days trying to persuade his brothers and nephews not to go. This time mother was proved right once again. The nine thousand men that assembled that scorching July day at Liberty Square were not taken away. Instead, they were made to sign up for forced labour. Some were humiliated and severely beaten by the German soldiers. Three of Lola's uncles and five male cousins were among the nine thousand men at the square. By the end of that day, her uncles were released because they were over thirty-five years of age. However, her cousins together with thousands of other young men were sent into forced labour. They were only released three months later, when the Jewish community paid a hefty ransom.

The events that took place at Liberty Square that July day were a terrible blow for the Jewish community of Salonica. The Nazis revealed their hatred and feelings for the Jews by exercising their authority in such a brutal manner.

Most Jews however, including Lola's father, still believed that the best thing to do was to lay low. No-one could have imagined that even more perverted and sinister events awaited them.

During the next couple of months, Lola tried to block out the unfolding thoughts deep within her mind by immersing herself in her cousin Rachelle's wedding. Lola and Rachelle's fathers were brothers. The two families had spent countless summers together and Lola was happier than ever because she was one of two bridesmaids. Her aunt, a seamstress by profession, made the wedding dress and the bridesmaid's dresses. Lola had never been more excited as she went once a week to Rachelle's house for a fitting. She always looked up to her cousin who was four years older and very beautiful. She was known to all her friends as Aphrodite[88] because she was tall and slender with dark blonde hair. In Lola's eyes her cousin was the epitome of beauty and Lola made no secret of wanting to look like her.

"You're beautiful too," said mother, whenever Lola complained. "In my eyes, you are much more beautiful than your cousin. You have thick dark hair, green eyes and let's not forget your pretty face."

Rachelle's wedding day finally arrived at the end of January. Despite the winter season, the weather was unusually mild with the Salonican sun shining all day. The ceremony took place at the only Synagogue still standing which was situated in a narrow lane. From the outside no-one knew it was a Synagogue. The Rabbi[89] conducted the ceremony with very ancient Sephardic traditions.

 The covering of the couple's heads with the talit was a mysterious custom that Lola found fascinating. Her father explained that this tradition symbolised that, in God's eyes, this is the moment when the couple are united and become one.

Once the ceremony ended, the guests exited from a side door into a small courtyard. Then, as the bride and groom came out, they were bombarded with sugar coated almonds and coins. The bride had her veil to protect her from the almonds but the groom would usually take a few to the head.

---

[88] The Greek goddess of love and beauty.
[89] *Hebrew* in Judaism, a Rabbi is a teacher of the Bible.

These traditions were brought by their forefathers from Toledo, when they came to Salonica hundreds of years ago.

The almonds symbolized the bitterness of life, and for this reason they were sugar coated, so that whatever obstacles they faced, sweetness would prevail.

The coins were a wish for prosperity for the rest of their lives.

Following this ancient tradition, the guests made their way to the reception hall, which was in the building across the street. However, they were told to leave the Synagogue in threes and to quietly make their way to the hall. These were unusual times and the loud hustle and bustle that was often seen in the streets of Salonica during a Jewish wedding had been forbidden under the Nazi occupation. The joyous wedding party were unaware of the fact that their occupiers were preparing to erase their every trace.

Chapter Three

The Dream

In February of 1943, Lola had a dream that Salonica was experiencing mild weather and the streets were filled with people going about their daily routines. Lola was on one of her usual walks holding a fresh bouquet of flowers that she had purchased from her local florist. She was headed to her Grandma Rachel's home. Arriving on Nikis Avenue she walked straight ahead towards the White Tower which stood tall like a defender of the city. From her earliest years at school she had learnt about this Salonican landmark. It had been built by the Ottoman Turks in the 15th century and had been used as a fortress for nearly four hundred years. In her dream, Lola gazed up at the Tower which suddenly began to fall. She was shocked. The White Tower was Salonica's pillar of strength. Nothing could ever bring it down and yet it was collapsing before her very eyes.

She turned and ran as quickly as she could, "O lefkos pirgos pefti[90]," she yelled at the top of her lungs. Lola woke up from the dream, breathing heavily and sweating profusely. It took her a few seconds to realise that she had been dreaming, for it wasn't spring at all, it was still early February. Lola lay there in silence thinking of how real the dream had been. Her mind went back to when the city was bombed by the Italians.

---

[90] *Greek* The White Tower is falling

She prayed to herself that the Germans would not bomb Salonica because if they did, she feared that the unthinkable would happen – that the indestructible white tower would fall.

Lola often had dreams that predicted the future and this made her afraid. She closed her eyes and tried to go back to sleep, hoping that when she awoke, this dream would be erased from her mind.

The following morning Lola went off to school. The first lesson that day was Geometry. She sat there waiting for the hour to pass as she despised the subject. She was looking forward to the next lesson which was Ancient Greek. It was by far her favourite subject as she indulged in the lives of the ancients through her books. She knew all of the Greek myths off by heart and had re-read, over and over again, Homer's books, 'The Odyssey' and the 'The Iliad'. At 9:25am just before the end of the first lesson, the Vice-Principal walked into the class and asked all the Jewish students to make their way to the school hall. Lola, with five other girls stood up and left as they had been instructed to do. As they entered the hall they saw that it was filling up with the school's Jewish students. They then sat quietly until the Principal came in to make an announcement.

"Girls, I have just been informed that I have to order you to leave immediately and it is with great regret that I tell you this. As you know, the Germans are in charge and they have given this order which we have to abide by," said Madame Ziskou as she held back her tears. "I am sure that when the war is over we will see you all again."

She and the Vice-Principal went to the door of the school and gave a brave smile to each girl as they walked out.

Lola hurried as quickly as she could back to her house. As soon as she entered, she saw her mother cutting up yellow material.

"What's going on?" asked Lola.

"Why are you home?" asked Rachel.

"We were told by the Principal that we had to come home."

"The Germans have issued an order," said Rachel. "All Jews have to wear a yellow 'Star of David[91]' on their clothing."

"Why?" asked Lola.

"So that we can be easily identified…"

"So that we can become easy targets for hoodlums to harass us," interrupted Moishe.

"Stop it," said mother. "I'm making a 'Star of David' for each one of us."

"Don't make one for me," said Rachel, "Because I refuse to wear something so humiliating."

"Me too," said Moishe.

"We're all going to wear it and that's final," said mother.

"That's what you think?" muttered Rachel under her breath, as she walked off.

Lola went up to the bedroom that she shared with her sister. "Is it true that you're not going to wear it?" asked Lola.

"Of course I'm not going to wear it. It's demeaning and humiliating."

"But it's the 'Star of David'. We should wear it with pride," said Lola.

---

[91] A six-pointed figure of two interlaced triangles, used as a Jewish and Israeli symbol. It represents the emblem on King David's shield during biblical times.

"You should wear with pride the gold 'Star of David' necklace that grandma bought you but not a piece of yellow material that's shaped as a star. They want us to wear it so that they can humiliate us. Don't you understand?" exclaimed Rachel.

Lola lay down on her bed, facing away from Rachel, so that she could hide the tears rolling down her cheeks. She thought back to her dream and was now beginning to understand its meaning. The White Tower may not have collapsed in reality but for Lola it was slowly tumbling before her eyes.

For the next month, Lola spent most of her time in her room, waiting to be allowed to go back to school. She had never had so much time off school and it felt so strange to her. All she could do was hope that things would get back to normal soon.

Her sister Rachel stubbornly refused to expose the yellow Star of David in public and always covered it up with her coat as she left the house. Sometimes she even removed the star and put it in her pocket. Her parents never knew that Rachel was doing this.

Just when the community was getting over the shock of having to wear the star, another troubling announcement was made. It was mid-March around eleven o'clock in the morning when Rachel entered the house looking flustered, with the star half-dangling from her lapel.

"We have to move into a ghetto within 48 hours," she said.

"What's that?" asked Lola hearing the word for the first time.

"It's a particular area in the city where all the Jews of Salonica have to move to."

"Where is this restricted area?" asked Lola.

"Near the railway station," said father as he entered the room.

"Which station?" asked mother?

"At the Baron Hirsch district," he replied.

"That area is completely run down," she said.

"We have no choice in the matter," said father. "For now we'll take what we can with us and in the next few weeks we'll slowly transport the rest of our belongings to our new home."

"How will we get there?" asked mother.

"On foot," replied father.

"What?" exclaimed mother. "It will take us at least two hours to get there."

"Like I said, we have no other choice. We have to abide by the law."

For the next two days, their mother was either crying or trying desperately to hold back her tears as she collected what she could. The family had an old horse cart which had not been used for a decade. They began loading it with the items they thought were necessary. Every hour that went by the cart was filling up. Lola spent most of her time in her bedroom trying to decide what to take with her.

"Don't worry," said Rachel. "My friend told me that she will try to find us a safe place outside of the ghetto."

"Christina?" asked Lola.

"Yes," replied Rachel, "Her father told her that they can put us up until the Germans leave."

"All of us?"

"No, only you and me," said Rachel. "Don't you get it?"

"Get what?"

"They're going to hide us in their home but they only have room for the two of us."

"I'm not going without mama and baba," said Lola.

"Listen," said Rachel, "They'll be fine. Occasionally we'll sneak into the ghetto to see them."

"Why don't we just stay with them?" she asked.

"Because Christina told me that the ghetto has already filled up. It will be completely cramped in a week's time. We'll be better off at her home."

Lola thought about it and realised it was a good idea, as long as she could see her parents as often as possible. She took out her small travel bag and began filling it up with her dresses. Just before she closed her bag, she grabbed her favourite Ancient Greek books which were five of Euripides[92] tragedies and packed them on top of her clothes.

The following morning at nine o'clock sharp, the Germans arrived in their neighbourhood. They went from house to house banging on everyone's front door.

"Raus, raus[93]," they yelled.

---

[92] An ancient Athenian writer of Greek tragedy.
[93] *German* Get out.

Lola's father opened the door, and with a heavy heart, led his family out of the house. Slowly and full of sadness, the Seror family made their way towards the Baron Hirsch district with Moishe pulling the horseless cart, laden with their belongings. Lola held her bag with her right hand and on her left side grandma Joya's arm was holding tightly onto hers. People stopped to stare at them while others looked away. Occasionally, the women would call out, "May God be with you."

After a strenuous, humiliating and exhausting two hours Lola and her family arrived at the railway station. The first thing they noticed was the barbed wire surrounding the area. There were three entrances to the ghetto but they had to walk another ten minutes to get to the closest one. Once inside the confines of the ghetto, Lola's father told the family to wait in a corner while he and Moishe went to look for an empty apartment. Nearly twenty minutes later father came back with grim news.

"I have managed to find just one empty room," he said.

"Beggars can't be choosers," said mother as she picked up her bag.

When they arrived at the building all that they noticed was broken windows and piles of rubbish.

"This is a strange looking hacienda[94]," said Lola.

"It's certainly not a hacienda," said Rachel. "It's just an abandoned warehouse."

The Baron Hirsch district had a few old warehouses that had been built by the Ottoman Turks. They had been deserted for many years and were swarming with rats and other pests.

---

[94] *Spanish* A large estate with a dwelling house.

Lola stared at the building in disgust.

"Don't just stand there," said Rachel, "Get a move on."

Lola walked as slowly as she could. She entered the building hesitantly, looking at all the cobwebs and dirt. At the back of the warehouse was a small room which was to become their temporary home. With no beds or any furniture, Lola and her family slept on the floor. That first night Lola hardly slept as she thought about the sudden changes in their circumstances. [Note: Lola's memories of the accommodation in the ghetto was very different from Maria's telling of the same scenario. This difference in memory is not unusual amongst Survivors who have been deeply traumatised.]

From the beginning of the German occupation, food had been scarce but for the next few weeks, the lack of food and burning hunger reached a new level.

One morning, Lola awoke to the sound of her mother's voice.

"She is burning up. We must get her to a doctor."

Lola's baby sister Arietta had fallen ill. With the damp room and the lack of food this was bound to happen. Rachel, Moishe and father spent the entire morning going from door to door in the ghetto searching for a doctor. At last, Rachel came across the Fernandez family whose father had his own medical clinic in downtown Salonica. He quickly made his way to the tiny Seror dwelling and proceeded to examine the child.

"How old is she?" he asked.

"Nearly fourteen months old," replied mother.

The doctor placed his stethoscope on Arietta's chest and on her back.

He examined her eardrums and took her temperature.

"She has a slight fever," he said. "Give her plenty of water and if you are able to, feed her a boiled egg once a day. I assure you that she will be better within a week."

"If we were in our own home we would be able to," said mother, "But here in this hell-hole, it's virtually impossible."

The next few days were extremely challenging for father, Rachel and Moishe. They had to somehow find a few eggs. Luck was on their side when, the following morning, Christina came to the ghetto to hand Rachel a letter through the barbed wire fence.

"Arietta is sick and we need eggs to help her to recover," said Rachel.

"I'll be back in three hours," said Christina.

She hurried off and returned a few hours later with the eggs.

Christina's family had always considered Rachel as a member of their own family. They did not hesitate to give her their last ten eggs.

Rachel headed back to their room and to her mother's surprise and relief, she gave her the eggs. For the next week, Lola was put in charge of boiling an egg every day. Dr. Fernandez had been right, as a week later Arietta was herself again.

As more people arrived in the ghetto, the families who had been there for a while were leaving. If your surname was posted on the wall with a date next to it, that meant that you were being deported. Lola's brother was the designated one to check every day. One morning precisely twenty-one days after they had entered the ghetto, Moishe came running in out of breath.

"Father's name is on the board! We are being transported the day after tomorrow."

"Thank God," said mother. "I can't take much more of this. Any place is better than here."

"I hope you're right," said father.

"But you told me that the Chief Rabbi made an announcement that we will be sent to Germany to work in a village. We will have jobs and our own homes again."

"Yes he did," said father. "So let's go in peace, *kai o theos voethos*[95]."

The following day went painfully slowly. Lola rearranged her travel bag at least four times. She made sure to include every single item that she had brought with her into the ghetto. She did not know how long before she could buy a new toothbrush or hair comb so she thought it best to take everything with her.

"Hopefully," she thought to herself, "Baba will earn enough so that I could shop from the stores in Germany."

As soon as she had fastened her bag, Rachel came to the door and motioned for Lola to come out.

"What's wrong?" asked Lola.

---

[95] *Greek* With God's guidance and assistance.

"Christina is waiting just outside the ghetto. She wants me to tell you for the last time not to go to Germany with the rest of the family but to stay here. Her family will keep us safe."

"I can't leave without mama and baba," said Lola. "Besides, we're going to be resettled somewhere in eastern Germany."

"Father Nikolas told me not to believe what the Germans are saying," said Rachel.

"But the Chief Rabbi of Salonica has said that they're taking us to a safe place. If you don't believe me ask baba."

"Okay," said Rachel, "Suit yourself."

"I don't know why you insist on staying," said Lola. "Mama and baba will never allow it."

Rachel looked at her sister and smiled. She turned around and left the room.

The following morning they awoke before the break of dawn. Lola was hot and sweating. She had a fever. There wasn't anything they could do as they had to leave. Mother took one of her woollen scarves and wrapped it around Lola's head.

"Don't take this off," said mother, "It will keep your head warm."

As they were doing their last minute packing Rachel came into the room.

"Christina gave me this loaf of bread to take with you. Who knows when your next meal will be?" she said.

"When did you see Christina?" asked father. "And where were you last night?"

"I spent the night with uncle Ephraim's family. Anyway, he told me I can leave with his family. They're leaving in two days."

"Are you sure you want to come with your cousins?" asked father.

"Yes, I'm sure," she replied.

Rachel embraced and kissed each member of her family.

"Be careful," said mother.

"I will," said Rachel.

"We'll see you in a few days," said Lola as she waved one last time to her sister before exiting the ghetto.

They made their way to the railway station which was a half hour walk. The platform was already full of people and as Lola glanced around she saw that even more people were arriving. With nowhere to sit they stood in silence, waiting for the train to arrive. In what seemed like an eternity, the train finally pulled into the station. Two German soldiers slid the doors open and a makeshift wooden ramp was put into place. Lola and her family boarded the train, one by one. Once aboard, they realised that these were not normal passenger trains. Lola's first instinct was to sit down but there was barely enough space in the already overcrowded cattle car. More and more people entered the wagon until it was filled to capacity. The majority were forced to stand as there was hardly room to move.

Lola curled up into a ball trying to get over the shock. She did not know what was worse, the fact that they were packed in like herrings or that there were no seats or toilet facilities on the train. There was nothing at all. The inhumanity of the situation was impossible to comprehend.

It wasn't too long before the train's whistle was heard and the carriages began to roll slowly along the tracks. Lola's brother squeezed down next to her.

"This is a train for horses," said Lola. "There are no windows or seats."

"There is one window," said Moishe as he motioned upwards with his head. Lola gazed up at the small window at the corner of the wagon.

"I'm right," she said. "It is a horse train."

During the next few hours complete silence engulfed the wagon. The only sound coming from inside the train was the crying of babies and the occasional whimper coming from Lola's sisters. Mathilde who was two and a half years old was lying in Lola's arms and Arietta who had just turned one was in her mother's arms. As the journey progressed, Lola began to lose track of time. It was difficult to breathe because they were all so cramped. But it was the overwhelming stench that she really couldn't deal with. She was constantly in and out of sleep as if she had been drugged.

Every now and again Lola's father cut tiny pieces from a loaf of bread that he had brought with him, and gave it to each member of his family. Lola chewed slowly on the piece of bread. She could see that the loaf was getting smaller.

After travelling for an indiscernible amount of time, the train came to a halt. One of the teenage boys in the wagon looked out of the window and saw that the train had stopped at a large train station.

"Can you see anything?" asked a tall grey haired man standing beside him.

"Yes," he replied. "I can see soldiers and a sign."

"What does the sign say?"

"It says Belgrade."

"We're still in Yugoslavia?" asked another man.

"Maybe now they'll open the doors so that we can get some air," said an ashen faced woman.

"Wait a moment," said Lola's father, "I have an idea."

He had taken with him an old straw covered retsina[96] bottle which he had filled up with water. However, after so many days on the train, the family had consumed every last drop. He went over to the small window and waved the bottle to one of the soldiers who was standing on guard. He wanted the bottle to be filled with water. Not for him but for his children, especially the two youngest who were exhausted and were beginning to look pale and sickly.

The soldier removed his rifle from his shoulder and swung it onto the bottle, smashing to pieces. Lola looked up at her father and the expression on his face was one of helplessness and desperation.

There was no way to tell how long the train remained standing there. Lola had closed her eyes and tried to sleep. Eventually, the train began moving and once again, the train became as silent as a grave, not a word from anyone. The horrendous conditions on the train had left many dead. Some still standing and others crumpled on the floor of the carriage. The space was so limited that many people had no option but to sit down on top of the corpses. This was the first time that Lola saw her father sit down. Lola

---

[96] Greek wine flavoured with resin.

sat on the cold wooden floor and found herself staring at a man very close to her. He slowly took out a small cup from his pocket. He then urinated in the cup. Lola was horrified and shocked when he began to drink his own urine. She felt like vomiting.

Lola then pressed her face against mother's soft arm.

"I feel sick," she said. "I want to use the rest room."

"Can you wait a bit longer?" said mother. "I'm sure we haven't got long to go."

"Mama, I can't take it anymore! We've been in this wagon for nearly three days."

"Try to sleep," said mother. "Try not to think of what makes you sad. I promise, we're nearly there now."

Lola did not know if her mother really knew that they would be arriving soon or if she was just saying that to make her daughter feel better.

Lola began to shiver. An iciness was coming from her right side. A middle-aged woman who had sat quietly next to her for the entire journey was now completely motionless with her eyes wide open. Lola stretched out her arm and touched her. She felt like a block of ice.

"Lola, don't look at her," whispered mother, "Her soul is in God's Kingdom now."

Lola then understood that the woman had died. A man who had been sitting next to the woman placed his hand over her face and closed her eyelids. He then began to recite the Kaddish – the Jewish prayer for the dead. When he was finished, he wept.

"Please," said mother. "Close your eyes and try to rest."

After a few attempts of trying to get to sleep, Lola once again pressed against her mother.

"I had this dream," she said. "Actually, it was more like a nightmare."

"When?" asked mother.

"A few weeks ago before we moved into the ghetto."

"Describe the dream to me," she said.

"I was walking along Nikis Avenue on my way to Grandma Rachel's home when in the distance I saw the White Tower collapse."

Lola felt a chill coming from her mother.

"Don't worry," she said. "The White Tower will never fall."

"But now that I am experiencing this hellish train journey, in my mind it has collapsed," said Lola.

"I told you we don't have long to go. When we arrive we will bathe and they will give us some food. The nightmare is nearly over."

Lola needed to believe that this torment would soon be over. The hours dragged on with no end in sight. Through the small opening they could see if it was day or night but after about six days, the few who were keeping count had lost track of time.

At long last the train came to a halt and everyone was shaken up by the loud shouts coming from outside of the train. Then the doors were abruptly flung open and the soldiers on the platform were shouting, "Raus! Schnell, schnell[97]. Leave your luggage behind."

---

[97] *German* Everybody out, quickly.

Slowly, people began to stand but many remained motionless on the wagon's wooden floor. Lola held onto Moishe's hand as she climbed over the dead bodies before jumping off the train. She looked around her and noticed a sign on the station platform. Against a white backdrop in bold capital letters, was the name of the town. Lola and her family had arrived at Auschwitz.

Chapter Four

Auschwitz-Birkenau 39403

(i) Arrival

The sight of men dressed in striped prison clothes was the first thing that Lola noticed on the station platform in the glaring daylight. Together with soldiers they forcefully began to separate everyone. They pulled people from one line to another. At the same time, through a loud speaker a voice with a foreign accent, repeated in Greek, "All men over sixteen and under fifty, go to the right side. Women with children and men over fifty go to the left. All women without children go to the far right." The screams of women and the cries of toddlers was deafening as Lola hovered close to her mother. The line began moving very slowly. Up ahead, Lola could see men dressed in white coats with stethoscopes around their necks. She assumed they were doctors and this made her feel safe. She knew they would be looked after. As they got closer, one of the men in a striped uniform with a familiar face whispered in her ear, "Tell the doctor you're sixteen."

"But I *am* sixteen," said Lola, as she stared at the familiar looking man with a Salonican accent. She knew him from somewhere but her mind had gone blank. Lola heard Grandma Joya ask the Salonican man, "Raoul, what will happen to us?"

"Don't worry Mrs. Capone, everything will be alright."

"Of course," muttered Lola under her breath, "It's Raoul." He looked unrecognisable due to his loss of weight and unkempt appearance. Raoul was cousin Lucia's brother. She was a cousin through marriage and very much loved in the Seror family.

Seeing a familiar face made her fear subside even more. She was convinced that they would have a chance to clean up, eat and rest.

Lola and her mother Emma stood expectantly in front of the doctor. He did not examine them but merely asked questions.

"How old are you?" asked the German doctor in heavily accented Greek.

"Forty-two," replied Lola's mother.

He then directed her to go to the right side.

"I want to stay with my mother and children," she said.

He nodded and Lola's mother did not move. The doctor then addressed Lola.

"How old are you?" he asked.

"Sixteen," replied Lola.

He then pointed for her to go to the right side, as well.

"But I want to stay here with my mother," she said.

A soldier grabbed Lola's arm and forcibly pulled her away as she desperately resisted.

"Mama," she cried.

"Lola," howled mother, as the desperate tone in her voice echoed together with all the other screams. Emma had been holding her daughter Arietta in her arms and she passed her to grandma Joya as she rushed out of the line to give Lola the woollen scarf which she had worn throughout their hellish journey. An SS guard pushed her roughly back into line. Lola looked back and saw her mother holding on to the woollen scarf. She began to run towards her mother when Raoul stopped her. He whispered in her ear, "You're too young to die."

Lola became paralysed with fear, thinking that she might be shot by one of the soldiers nearby. She stood there motionless in her line, all alone amongst strangers. Lola was frightened and shivering. She cautiously looked around the station platform and spotted her father and brother who were staring at her. She suddenly felt calm. A loud whistle blew and the line she had been in before began to move forward.

Lola looked to her right and saw both her grandmothers with her mother and two little sisters walk by. They were not looking anywhere but straight ahead. They looked totally exhausted. Lola hoped that in a little while they would be given some food and would be allowed to rest. She remained calm, believing that she would see them again very soon. Another whistle blew and her line began to move. She began walking, blindly following the person in front of her. She was not in control of her destiny anymore. After walking for some time, they arrived at a camp with big iron gates. They moved past the gates, following the soldiers. They reached a room where women wearing striped prison uniforms pulled them out of line to remove eyeglasses or jewellery. Lola was quickly checked and pushed along as she had neither of these things on her. The line slowed down and then stopped. Each woman was forced to sit on a chair and one of the prisoners was writing something on their forearms. When it was her turn, Lola realised that it wasn't a pen but a needle with ink. It seemed to take forever and the pain was unbearable. She could see blood and blue ink running down the side of her arm. Her arm was wiped over with a cloth and then she was pushed out of her chair and forced to move along again. They were ordered to remove all of their clothes. Lola obeyed without thinking. Once she removed her dress, a woman prisoner began to remove her petticoat but Lola resisted as she was embarrassed to be naked. The woman forcefully lifted her petticoat up and pulled it off. She was left standing in her underwear and was feeling deeply humiliated as she was motioned to remove all her clothing. The woman threw the clothes into a big cauldron. Lola was pushed towards a long bench where other women were seated and had to sit alongside them. Eventually she was forced to sit on a chair and as she sat there, naked, her hair was cut by a female prisoner, with a pair of clippers. Her long thick locks were shaved down to her scalp. This awful process didn't end there as she was then ordered to stand on two chairs with her legs spread apart, while her pubic hair and underarm hair was shaved off by a male prisoner. This was excruciatingly embarrassing for Lola. Once again she was pushed along into another room where warm water was running from the shower heads. They were given a bar of soap and she quickly washed her bruised, naked body alongside the other women. With no towel to dry themselves, they were marched outside into the chilly late afternoon air. They were forced to stand up straight as a male prisoner dipped a huge brush into a bucket and then smeared the liquid all over each woman's body. The stinging and burning sensation of the strong solution was very painful. For the first time, tears rolled down Lola's cheeks as she stood naked amongst strangers. The women were marched to another building where they were given a striped uniform and clogs. Lola's uniform was too big and the clogs were too small but she didn't care anymore. For the first time in her life she just wanted to die.

The group then stood in a line where they were each given a piece of bread. Lola practically swallowed it whole. The sun began to set as they were taken to their barracks which was to become their sleeping quarters. Upon entering they saw a big room filled with bunks that were already occupied. They were led to the bunks by female kapos[98] with batons in their hands.

Five women were allocated to every empty bunk. Lola was the first to climb up to the wooden bunk which was covered with straw. There were no mattresses, no blankets, nothing. During the many cold nights, Lola was glad to feel the other women's bodies providing her with warmth. However, during the hot summer months it was nothing more than hell, as she found herself waking up in the middle of the night gasping for air.

---

[98] Nazi concentration camp prisoners who were given privileges in return for supervising forced labour.

During her first night, despite her exhaustion, Lola found it hard to sleep. A million things were going through her mind as she lay there frightened and shivering from the cold.

"God, where have you brought us to?" she muttered under her breath as she closed her eyes and thought about her parents, her grandmothers, her brother and two little sisters. She had decided, as she lay there, that in the morning she would try to find them.

Squeezed amongst the other women she lifted her left arm and for the first time that evening, she looked carefully at the engraved pale-blue tattoo. She saw that it was a number, *39403*. This was now her new identity. She touched it tentatively with her right hand. The pain from the needle had not yet subsided and the imprint was swollen. She put her arm down and began to sob as quietly as she could. The woman facing her whispered in Greek,

"Don't cry my young girl."

Lola's tears instantly stopped.

"What's your name my young one?"

"Lola. And you?"

"My name is Elli."

For the first time in a very long time, Lola smiled.

"Don't worry," said Elli, "I will look after you."

"Where are you from?" asked Lola.

"Larissa," she replied.

"Did you come with your family?" asked Lola.

"I came with my parents, but we were separated. Tomorrow God willing, we will look for them. Now try to get some sleep."

Lola nodded as she shut her tired eyes.

The deafening sound of a whistle is what woke Lola the next morning.

Two kapos went around pushing the women to get up. They yelled at them and used their batons to shock them out of their sleep.

Lola jolted up and jumped down from the bunk with Elli's help.

"Today we will search for our families," she whispered in Lola's ear.

As they made their way outside, Lola saw a terrible scene around her. She saw men and women walking around with swollen feet and hands. She was taken aback by this ghastly sight. They looked like animals.

"What's wrong with them?" she asked Elli.

"It's the hunger that did this to them, they are starving."

All of a sudden she became extremely frightened and all she wanted was to leap into her mother's arms and feel that security that she longed for.

"When will we look for my mother and father?"

"Very soon," replied Elli. "Wait here and I will go and ask those women who arrived before us."

Lola stood there in the crisp morning air. Suddenly a whistle blew. She heard one of the kapos yelling out, "Appell, appell[99]."

As she didn't speak German she could not understand what it meant but she saw the other prisoners beginning to form lines. Lola slipped into the closest line. It didn't take long to understand what was happening. The guards began counting each prisoner. It was a very slow process that

---

[99] *German* Roll call.

seemed to take forever. Eventually, when it was over, the girl next to Lola said, "Today it was short. Yesterday they had us standing here for nearly two hours." This girl had already been there for a week and she was also from Salonica.

Did she say 'short' Lola asked herself, because to her it felt like an eternity. She didn't want to think about that right now. All she could think of was seeing her family again. She looked around trying to find Elli who had told her she was going to try to discover the whereabouts of their families. She seemed to have vanished.

Another Salonican girl approached Lola and said, "If you want breakfast, you need to have your own bowl. Go inside and find one."

Lola followed some other girls who were grabbing bowls for themselves. As she went to take one, she noticed that the bowl in front of her was filled with faeces. She turned to the side and vomited. She knelt down coughing and vomiting at the same time. It was all too much for her. Lola had lost her appetite and all she wanted to do it was lie down. Her nausea was unbearable. But she knew she couldn't stay there forever. She slowly got up and made her way outside. As she looked to her right, there in the corner just outside the barrack was Elli, curled up in a ball.

"What happened," said Lola, as she knelt down beside her. Elli was sobbing. She was inconsolable. Lola was too afraid to find out why, so she hugged her and stroked her head. Then, the whistle blew. The guards and the kapo women were yelling out in what seemed to Lola's ears, to be an unfamiliar and barbaric language.

A female SS guard with a baton hit Lola across the back. Lola rushed to stand in line. The SS guard then hit Elli but she remained there motionless. By now her tears had dried up. As Lola watched from the corner of her eye she prayed desperately to God to make Elli get up. But God was nowhere to be seen. The guard continued to beat Elli relentlessly, as if a demonic spirit had possessed her. She beat her and beat her until Elli was lying in a pool of blood.

Lola was churning inside and once again she could not prevent herself from vomiting. The whistle blew again and like a dead woman walking, she followed the line. Lola felt completely emotionally paralysed. She was unable to comprehend that the girl from Larissa who had shown such kindness to her the night before, had been so cruelly and inhumanely beaten to death. As they approached the front gate of the camp, Lola could hear an orchestra playing. The musicians were female prisoners who played the most beautiful music. She could see violinists and cello players, all with dark circles around their eyes, completely expressionless. She was now convinced that this was hell. Someone had once told her, in what now seemed to be another lifetime, that even Satan has the urge to fill his soul with beautiful music.

As they walked through the wrought iron gateway, for a split second, Lola thought of running away. But her good sense took over and she knew that she would either be shot or be beaten to death just like Elli. She so desperately wanted to see her mother. She swore to herself that as soon as they returned to the camp, she would immediately begin searching for her.

After walking for some time, they arrived at a big vacant lot that was covered with mounds of soil. They each had to fetch a shovel and were ordered to begin digging. They were forbidden to look up even for a moment. Lola dug with ferocity as her anger had overcome her. The nameless Salonican girl from earlier, whispered quietly, "Don't waste your energy. You won't be able to go on for long."

"I don't care anymore," replied Lola.

"Do you want them to shoot you so you can fall into this hole that we are digging, because that's what will happen to you?"

Lola realised she could be shot at any moment if she stopped digging. She continued at a slower pace, thinking about her mother and how she wanted to feel her comforting arms around her. This first day of hard labour was one of the toughest days of her life. The thought of having to do this all day without a break was unbearable but it was the thought of seeing her family again that got her through it.

Once again the whistle blew and they were ordered to stop. Lola had completely lost track of time. They lined up and began the half hour march back to the camp. At this stage, there were two things on Lola's mind, seeing her mother again and having something to eat.

Once they re-entered the camp, Lola approached one of the girls who had been there for a while.

"Please," she said, "Can you help me find my mother and father? I haven't seen them for two days."

The young lady looked at her with a baffled expression on her face. The Salonican girl, who had now become her friend, came up from behind Lola and placed her arm around her.

"You haven't told me your name," she said.

"My name is Lola, Lola Seror."

"And my name is Mathilde Venezia. You're from Salonica just like I am." Lola nodded.

"What part of Salonica?"

"Please Mathilde," said Lola, "I just want to find my family. One of my little sisters has your name. You can meet her once I have found them." Mathilde Venezia had a very difficult job on her hands. She had the most daunting, unfathomable task that anyone could have, and that was to explain to this naïve, innocent girl that her family had been ruthlessly murdered. Gassed upon arrival. It took a few moments for Lola to comprehend what was coming out of Mathilde's mouth. It seemed so ridiculous, so incomprehensible, that Lola began to think that Mathilde may have been losing her mind.

"What do you mean, they were gassed?" asked Lola.

"They did not have a shower as they were told, but rather they were gassed."

"Please Mathilde," implored Lola, "Stop being cruel. I can't take it anymore."

Lola began to sob, "Please just help me find them."

"I didn't want to tell you this, but it's true. My family were also gassed. At first, I refused to believe it as well. But now I know that it's true."

"But I saw them walk by me," said Lola.

"Who did you see?" asked Mathilde.

"My grandmothers, my mother and my two little sisters. They passed me on their way to the bath house."

"It's not really a bath house," said Mathilde, "They're gas chambers."

For a brief moment Lola remained silent as she tried to get her head around the reality of the tragic situation. Then without warning, she began yelling out hysterically, "But why… why… what did we ever do to them? My mother and sisters are innocent. They never hurt anyone. How could they do this to us?"

Lola collapsed to the ground and with Mathilde's arms around her, she sobbed and sobbed uncontrollably.

That evening, Lola went without food, but it didn't seem to bother her, as her stomach ached with sorrow and loss.

Mathilde, who had now become Lola's protector, had kept half of the slice of her bread and offered it to Lola later on. She refused it.

"Lola, tomorrow you must eat. You can't go on another day without any food. You will become ill."

"What about my father?" asked Lola.

Mathilde looked down, before saying, "Lola you're not alone. My family was murdered too."

For most of that night, Lola stared blankly ahead of her. She could not sleep. She was numb, emotionally and physically. Eventually she fell into a fitful slumber.

The following morning Lola was once again awoken by the shouts of the female kapos who used their whips to wake up the girls. As she climbed down from her bunk she felt a deep nausea. She knew that her stomach was crying out for a bit of food. This time, once *appell* was over she was one of the first to run in and get a bowl. She then queued up for her first morning coffee at Auschwitz. It didn't look like the percolated coffee her parents brewed at home. It looked more like dirty hot water, but she didn't care. She drank it all down and then she ate the tiny piece of black bread that she was given.

"It's not real coffee," whispered Mathilde.

"I don't care," said Lola, "It's better than nothing."

"They call it *ersatzkaffee*[100]. It's most likely made from acorns."

Lola continued to chew her tiny piece of bread.

"How about the bread, is this not real too?" asked Lola.

"My sister found out from one of the male prisoners that sawdust is put in the dough."

"What?" asked Lola, as she continued chewing.

"To fill it up, because the flour is limited."

Lola did not care. It was a far cry from her days in Salonica when she was an extremely fussy eater. As far as she was concerned they could have filled up the flour with sand from the dunes of Africa, she would still have

---

[100] *German* Substitute coffee not made from coffee beans. The replacement is of poorer quality.

eaten it. Hunger is something she had never experienced but now after so many days on an empty stomach it began to hurt.

As they stood there finishing their meagre meal, a tall slim girl appeared next to Lola.

"This is Lambrini," said Mathilde, "My younger sister."

Lola half smiled as did Lambrini.

Mathilde and Lambrini were known as 'the two Greek sisters of Birkenau'. They were warm and kind but also ruthless if they needed to be in order to survive. They were the only two from their family to be selected for labour. Everyone else was sent to the gas chambers.

"I need to go to the toilet" said Lola.

"Hurry quickly," said Mathilde, the whistle will blow very soon.

This was Lola's second day in Auschwitz but as yet she had not used the latrines to empty her bowels. After inspecting them on her first day, she was hoping she wouldn't have to, but nature caught up with her and she had no choice but to go. In a big room behind the barracks there was a long bench with ten holes, one next to the other and ten buckets positioned under the holes. There was absolutely no privacy as the women sat next to each other, feeling humiliated. They had been forced to live like animals. There was no other way.

Once she was done, Lola quickly made her way outside only to trip over a dead body that had fallen from a big pile of skeletal corpses that were stacked one on top of the other waiting to be taken to the crematoria to be burnt. She hurriedly got up and avoided the corpse's face.

Lola would never become immune to these images during her next two years in Auschwitz and they would stay with her forever.

Chapter Four

(ii) The Weekly Selections

One week had passed since Lola's arrival at Birkenau. The days seemed to get longer but the nights were very cold. She would shiver during the night, and even the other women's bodies didn't warm her up anymore. If only she had a blanket to cover herself, it would make such a difference. Her thoughts were constantly transported back to Salonica where she had a warm bed with woolly blankets. A necessity in life that she had taken for granted. These thoughts consumed her so much that she even had dreams about it. On her sixth night Lola had the most vivid of these dreams. She was back at home in the basement and her mother was taking all the blankets upstairs. They were very old but still looked new, some even dated back to two hundred years ago. Most of them were from Turkey. Her forefathers had travelled a number of times from Salonica to Constantinople[101] bringing back beautiful things. Once the blankets were upstairs, her mother hung them over the balcony and banged them with a broom to get rid of the dust. Lola was standing next to her mother helping her, holding up the blankets. All of a sudden part of the balcony railing seemed to have vanished. Her mother cautioned her to be careful. She took the broom from her mother and began beating the blankets. Suddenly she

---

[101] Constantinople was the capital city of the Byzantine Empire (330-1453) and the later Ottoman Empire (1453-1923). The modern Turkish name for the city, Istanbul, derives from the Greek phrase 'into the city'.

tripped and stumbled through the open part of the balcony. She fell and fell but never reached the ground. She landed on a number of woollen blankets stacked one on top of the other. She was shaken but unhurt.
Lola snapped out of her dream as she awoke to the morning shouts of the female kapos. As she rushed to the latrine, she remembered every detail of her dream. Lola hurried outside where everyone had lined up for appell. The wait that morning was unbearable as they were counted three times over. Then with the sound of the whistle, the lines were instantly dispersed and Lola immediately ran in to secure an unsoiled bowl. As she ate her piece of black bread and drank the dirty-watery coffee, she realised that they weren't being hurried as usual. She looked around and saw that some of the girls were sitting and others were standing holding their bowls, as if they had all day. Mathilde came and stood next to her.

"What's going on?" asked Lola, "Why haven't they shuffled us off to work?"

"Today is our day of rest," replied Mathilde.

"You mean once a week we have a day off?"

"For some of us it's our day off, and for others it's their last."

"What do you mean by that?"

"You'll soon find out," said Mathilde as she made her way into the barracks only to return with the tiniest of pins.

"What is that?" asked Lola.

"Here, take this and prick your finger."

"Why?" asked Lola.

Mathilde then took a deep sigh, before telling Lola what takes place on this day on a weekly basis.

"Today is blocksperre[102]."

"What does that mean?"

"It means that..."

Suddenly a female SS Officer blew the whistle and ordered everybody standing outside to go into the barrack. Once all the prisoners had gone in, the door was closed and bolted.

"What's going on?" asked Lola.

"Today is blocksperre," replied Mathilde, "We are not allowed to leave the barrack for the entire day."

Lola continued staring at her with a strange look in her eyes.

"The weekly selections take place on this day," continued Mathilde, "We are all going to be inspected by camp doctors."

"So can I lie down until they come?" asked Lola.

Mathilde nodded. She was restraining herself from telling Lola the full story as she could see that Lola, for a split second, was happy that she had a day off. Lola then motioned to Mathilde to lie on the bunk as well.

"Why did you ask me earlier to prick my finger?" asked Lola.

"So that you can rub some blood on your cheeks... you know, to look healthy in the doctor's eyes."

Lola agreed that was a good idea until she wondered if it would be better if they thought she was sick.

"But wouldn't it be better if they did think I was sick?" asked Lola.

---

[102] *German* Forbidden to leave the barrack.

Mathilde looked away choosing to remain silent.

"Are you still there?" whispered Lola.

"Yes," replied Mathilde, "I just have a splitting headache."

"Do you know when the doctors will come?" asked Lola.

"They have to pass through many blocks before they come to ours. It could be in a few hours, or at the end of the day," said Mathilde.

Lola then closed her eyes and tried not to think of anything Instead she just wanted to take this time to rest. She had been in the camp for one week already and her exhaustion had caught up with her. Then just as she had dozed off, Lola was awoken by the shouts of the SS female guards who opened the door and began shouting.

"Everybody get up," yelled the SS guards.

"Come on," screamed the female kapos as they hit the women, for most of them had been lying on their bunks.

Lola and Mathilde jumped down and lined up one behind the other.

They were first ordered to strip naked. They removed all their clothing and left it on the ground. They then filed slowly past the medical examiners. Two were seated at a table and another two stood behind them. The four of them wore white doctor's robes and some of them had stethoscopes around their necks, despite not ever using them. As Lola waited in line she could see that the SS doctor would either motion to the prisoner to move on or would take their left arm and write down their tattooed number. Lola understood from what Mathilde had told her that the doctors recorded the tattooed number only if they thought you were sick. As they approached the table, Mathilde was looked up and down and then motioned to pass.

Then it was Lola's turn. She took a couple of steps forward and stopped just in front of the doctors. They began staring at her body. She felt extremely embarrassed that the four men were looking at her private parts, even though they were doctors. To her relief one of them motioned for her to go by. She quickly put her prisoners uniform back on and then went and stood next to Mathilde who was anxiously waiting for her sister to pass the examination. Once Lambrini had passed the medical test, the sisters embraced as Lola looked on.

"How far is the medical clinic?" asked Lola.

"Why do you ask?" replied Mathilde.

"Because at future medical examinations if they take my number down I want to know how far the hospital is," she said.

Mathilde and Lambrini then looked at each other. They both knew that someone had to tell Lola.

"Lola, there is something I have to tell you," said Mathilde as she put her arm around her.

Lola stared at her quizzically.

"Every week when the doctors come here and examine us, those that they deem too sick…"

"Yes I know," interrupted Lola, "Their number is recorded."

"Yes it is," she said, "But afterwards they are not sent to the hospital."

"Then where do they take them?" she asked.

"To the gas chamber."

"You mean those who fail the medical exam are put to death?"

"Yes," replied Mathilde, "Every single day, hundreds and hundreds of people are sent to the gas chambers because they are physically too weak."

Lola took a few seconds to try to conceptualize what she had just heard.

"You mean if they had taken my number down, I would be sent to the gas chamber."

Mathilde nodded.

"That's why I told you earlier to prick your finger so you could smear your cheeks with some blood. Because if you have rosy cheeks…"

"Yes I know," said Lola, "The healthier you look the better your chances are."

Lola sat down on one of the bottom bunks. She was reeling from what she had just heard. In a way, she wished she hadn't been told the truth about the medical examination. From now on she knew that once a week she would have to live through the fear of not knowing if it was to be her last day on earth.

That evening, as Lola lay on her bed next to Mathilde and Lambrini she could hear the crying of the girls who were placed in the little room next to the barrack. Those poor souls who had their number recorded were placed in a sealed room. They would have to wait until the middle of the night to get picked up by the truck that would take them to the gas chambers and crematoria where their corpses would be incinerated once they were gassed.

"The truck comes very late," whispered Lambrini, "I've always been asleep when it has come to pick up the…"

"Shhh, try to sleep," said Mathilde, "Tomorrow it's back to digging."

Lola shut her eyes and tried to forget about what had transpired that day. However the whimpering of the girls in the little room kept her awake for a while. When she awoke in the morning, she realised that she had not been awake when the truck had come by during the night.

The next week went by fast, too fast for Lola because she didn't want Monday to arrive. But she knew she had no way out. On Monday morning the doctors arrived early. They set up the table and took their places as all the girls lined up naked waiting to be inspected like pieces of contaminated meat. As Lola stood in line, she stared at the three doctors who were present that day. Two were sitting behind the table and one was standing. When it came to Lola's turn she completely stiffened up. One of the doctors forcefully opened her jaw and looked with efficient precision inside her mouth. Then he pulled her arms up and looked underneath them. He turned and said something to the other two doctors in German. Lola did not understand. She was standing there for thirty seconds but it felt like an hour as they spoke amongst themselves, staring at her at the same time. One of the doctors pointed with his finger for Lola to move to the side. A female SS guard motioned for her to sit on a wooden bench. She did as she was told and just waited, naked, cold, and uncertain about whether it was time for her to die. Once they had examined all of the women one of the SS guards came over to her and lifted her chin with his hand. He examined her face and gave her the all clear by motioning for her to move on. She walked quickly back to where the piles of clothes lay and she hurriedly got dressed. Lambrini came from behind and led her away.

"From now on, you must prick your finger and smear your cheeks with your blood. It's not a guarantee that you will be spared but it reduces your chances of being selected."

Lola nodded and began to tremble. She knew that it had been a close call. From then on, every Sunday night Lola mentally prepared herself for the worst. What got her through the ordeal was the belief that, if she was selected to die, she would soon be with her Creator. She was not under any illusions. Facing the reality of the situation was her way of surviving.

After a month in the camp, she had changed within. If not for Auschwitz maybe she would never have reached this level of understanding of life but as fate had it, she was forced to. She had gone from being a naïve, happy girl to becoming a shrewd, calculating individual who would do her utmost to survive. This strength that she gained over the weeks became handy as the day arrived when she needed to be very strong to support her newly acquired friend whose worst nightmare became a reality.

Precisely one month after her arrival, on a chilly Monday morning, as soon as appell was over Lola lined up for a stale piece of bread and the ersatzkaffe.

"My sister doesn't feel well," said Lambrini standing behind Lola.

"What do you think is the matter?" asked Lola.

"She looks pale and she told me she's not hungry."

"She has to eat something," said Lola.

"Why today?" asked Lambrini anxiously, "She was fine all week. Today it's blocksperre and she has to look well for the medical examination."

"Don't worry," said Lola, "I have an idea."

Lambrini stared at her and was desperate to hear what Lola had to say.

"Once they open the doors and the SS have come inside the barrack," said Lola, "You and your sister can sneak out holding a bucket that needs emptying. They won't stop you. Just make sure not to come back until the doctors have left."

"But my sister won't be able to lift the bucket," said Lambrini.

"Take a half-empty one," said Lola. She was quite certain that no one would look into the bucket to see if it was full because of the foul odour.

That afternoon when the SS arrived, Lambrini and Mathilde were waiting with the half-filled bucket. They lifted the bucket as soon as the SS came inside the barrack. The female kapo who was behind the SS doctors motioned for them to quickly go and empty the bucket. They did not return until one hour later.

In the coming weeks, Lambrini, Mathilde and Lola took turns in emptying the bucket during the medical selections.

One day the female kapo realised what was going on and when Mathilde and Lola returned with an empty bucket, she began yelling at them and hit them a few times with her baton.

The following week it was Lambrini and Lola's turn to empty the bucket. Once the doors opened the female kapo glared at them and immediately approached an SS doctor and pointed at the girls. With his hand he motioned for them to go. They had been given the all clear. This continued for a few weeks until the day when Mathilde was not able to get out of bed let alone carry a half-filled bucket.

Lambrini was beside herself all morning not knowing what to do.

"I'll make sure that your sister's cheeks are extra rosy," said Lola as she put her arm around Lambrini.

She then pricked her finger and smeared extra blood on Mathilde's cheeks.

"You don't want it to look like rouge," said Lambrini, "Wipe some of it off."

Mathilde sat there motionless, breathing heavily. The barrack doors swung open and the kapos and female SS guards began shouting at the women to hurry up and get undressed. They all lined up, one behind the other, waiting to hear their fate. Lola was ushered through quickly by one of the SS doctors. Next, it was Mathilde's turn. The doctor opened her jaw and then looked under her arms. He looked at the other doctors. One of them nodded and turned Mathilde's arm over to record her number. Lambrini, who had been standing directly behind her sister, began pleading with the doctors. She did not speak German so she begged them in Ladino and Greek. She even knelt on the ground pleading with them. They were unmoved. The female SS guard who was standing by began to beat Lambrini and then grabbed her arm and pulled her away from the doctors. Lola found Lambrini's clothes and helped her sobbing friend to get dressed.

"Stop crying," said Lola, "Do you want them to take you away too?"

"Yes, I do," she cried, before realising that Mathilde was nowhere to be seen.

"I have to find my sister, where is she?"

"Sit down," said Lola pushing her onto one of the bottom bunks. "Listen to me. Next week it could be us. If it is, then I guarantee you that you will see your sister again very soon. But until that time comes you must be strong. You must make every effort to go on."

For the rest of that day Lambrini was inconsolable. Lola stayed with her holding her in her arms.

In the evening, they huddled together as they tried to sleep. By now, Lambrini had stopped sobbing. She just lay there staring vacantly in front of her. The women's cries from the little room next to the barrack could be heard. Lola wondered if one of those crying was Mathilde. She began praying, asking God to make Mathilde's death as painless as possible. Lola fell into a fitful sleep and was woken in the morning by the shouts of the kapo women. As she stood outside during appell she thought of Mathilde and knew that she was dead. She reached out and took Lambrini's hand. She held it tight and all morning did not let go. For the next few weeks, Lola watched as Lambrini withered away, until the morning when she refused to wake up. She had died in her sleep of a broken heart.

After Lambrini's death, Lola felt very alone. Sunday nights were the worst as she would fall asleep asking herself, "Am I leaving tomorrow?" Mondays were still her most challenging day. On those days the entire barrack was engulfed in silence. No one spoke, waiting, wondering if this time tomorrow they would be dead. It was an emotional hell that Lola had to endure for twelve long months and she would never be able to forget that fear.

Chapter Four

(iii) Rachelle

Five weeks after Lola had arrived at Auschwitz, on a cold Monday afternoon, she was lying on her bunk as it was *Blocksperre* day and the selection had already finished. There had been talk in the barracks about the arrival of new prisoners. In the past month many girls in Lola's barrack had either died or were selected for the crematoria, so everyone assumed that there would be an influx of new prisoners. A Greek girl, who later was sent to the crematorium, approached Lola and whispered to her that she had heard that some of the new arrivals were Greek. Lola didn't seem to take notice as she didn't think she'd know anyone. Later that evening when the prisoners were at rest, the silence was disturbed when a Kapo flung open the door.
"Hurry up," she yelled, as a group of new arrivals staggered in looking lost and confused. The women tried to find a space on a bunk.
"Five to a bunk," yelled the Kapo, "Move to make room for the new ones."
Lola could not believe it. For the past ten days she was down to sharing her bunk with one other girl but now three more had to squeeze in once again.
Within moments three new bodies lay on Lola's bunk and they all tried to be as comfortable as humanly possible. As soon as the lights were switched off the crying began. Some of the new girls had been in such

shock that it wasn't until they were lying in the dark amongst strangers, that they became fully aware of the reality of no longer being in control of their destiny.

One of the new girls who was pressing against Lola's back, began praying in Ladino. Lola could not resist and had to talk to her.

"Are you Greek?" she asked.

There was a moment's silence before the girl spoke.

"Yes," she replied softly.

"Where are you from?"

"Salonica."

"So am I," whispered Lola as the entire barrack was now falling silent.

"What's your name?" asked Lola.

"Ariadne. What's your name?"

"Lola, Lola Seror."

"Did you say Seror?" asked the new girl.

"Yes," replied Lola.

"Are *you* Rachelle's cousin?"

"Which Rachelle?" asked Lola in surprise.

"Rachelle Trapero."

Lola remained quiet for a few moments before quizzically replying.

"Yes, she *is* my cousin. But how do you know me?"

"I remember you at her wedding. Weren't you a bridesmaid?"

"Yes, I was," replied Lola, "How come you were there?"

"Rachelle is my good friend. We graduated from High School together."

"I see," whispered Lola.

"Your cousin is here, somewhere in this room," whispered Ariadne.

Lola sat in shocked silence.

"Lola, can you hear me?"

"Yes," replied Lola, "Are you sure it's my cousin?"

"I'm quite sure," she replied.

"Were you on the same transport?" asked Lola.

"Yes we were," she replied. "Tomorrow you'll be able to see her."

Lola spent a very restless night squashed up in her bunk. All she could think of was her cousin Rachelle's wedding day. And although it had only taken place three months earlier, it now seemed like a lifetime away.

In the morning, as soon as they were woken up by the kapos, Lola ran to the latrine, as she had not used it for over twelve hours. When she was finished, she noticed a familiar looking face of someone vomiting in one of the other latrines. She stopped and took a good look at this girl's profile. Despite the lack of hair Lola recognised her as her beloved cousin Rachelle.

"Rachelle," said Lola.

The girl looked up and with Lola's help she stood and embraced Lola warmly.

"I can't believe you're here," said Lola.

"Oh Lola," said Rachelle as she began to sob.

"Don't worry, I'm here, I will look after you," said Lola as they made their way outside and stood in line next to each other, ready for appell.

For the rest of the day, Lola and Rachelle stuck to each other like glue trying to talk whenever they could. On that first day, Rachelle had two pieces of news for Lola. She told her how her sister Rachel had never left Salonica. All she knew was that Rachel had gone into hiding. How and where, she had no clue. Lola was convinced that her sister was hiding at her best friend Christina's house. Rachel and Christina were inseparable. Lola felt so relieved and overjoyed to learn that at least there was one member of her family who was still alive back home. Rachelle's second piece of news was that of her pregnancy. She was four weeks pregnant, and all she could think of was her husband who had been separated from her on their arrival.

The following few days were extremely difficult for Lola as she had the task of explaining to her cousin the routines and daily life of Birkenau. Every fibre of her being told her not to say anything but she knew that Rachelle would soon find out anyway. The workings of the gas chambers, the crematoria and the dreaded weekly selections were something that Lola explained slowly and gently.
"What about Iakov?" asked Rachelle frantically.
"I do not know where your husband is but I will try to find out. He was probably chosen to work," said Lola even though she herself did not quite believe that.

Over the next few days Lola tried desperately to relay a message to the men's barracks, to try to find out if Iakov Trapero was there. Waiting for a reply was excruciating but all they could do was ask and wait. Then one day a male Jewish prisoner from Salonica came into the women's barracks to fix a water pipe in the wash room. Lola wasted no time in approaching him and asking about her cousin's husband. He told her that he had never heard of Iakov Trapero. Lola reassured her cousin Rachelle that no news is good news.

As the weeks went by, Rachelle's condition deteriorated. Once she had been the beauty queen of Salonica but now she was quickly becoming unrecognisable. Her demise made Lola think back to when a gypsy had once foretold Rachelle's fate.

It was in the summer of '39 when Lola and her cousins were at their holiday home on the Kassandra coast. One evening in mid-August, Lola and Rachelle attended the local fair which ran every Sunday during the summer. As they went by the stalls Lola had an idea. She so wanted to visit the gypsy's stall as she was known to give accurate predictions of one's *moirai*[103].

"I'm a little bit scared," said Rachelle, "My mother told me that gypsy predictions are not of God."

"Don't be silly," said Lola, "My father insists that we get our fortune told, it's all part of the fun."

Both girls approached the gypsy stall and waited patiently for their turn. Soon, the gypsy motioned with her head for the girls to approach her.

"Sit down," she said, "It will cost you a drachma each."

The girls paid the gypsy and then she asked who wanted to go first.

---

[103] *Greek* One's fate.

"I will," said Lola.

The gypsy took her right hand and pointed out the long life that she will have.

"This line shows that you will live to be very old."

The gypsy then gazed intensely at Lola's forehead.

"I can see it on your cross," said the gypsy.

"What cross?" asked Lola.

"The one on your forehead. It shows that you will marry in a foreign country and that you will live for most of your life in a land which is at the edge of the world."

Lola wasn't too sure what to make of it. She did not want to marry anywhere but in Salonica and she most certainly did not want to live in a faraway land. But she took it all in her stride and she reminded herself that it was all in fun.

Then it was Rachelle's turn and the gypsy went to grab her hand but Rachelle pulled back.

"Don't be frightened," said the gypsy.

"Please don't tell me anything bad," said Rachelle.

The gypsy nodded as Rachelle hesitantly extended her arm. The fortune teller gently took Rachelle's right hand and began to study her palm. The gypsy looked as though she was in a trance and was silent for at least a full minute as Lola and her cousin looked at each other.

"What can you see?" asked Rachelle, "Am I going to get married?"

"Yes," replied the gypsy.

"In Salonica?"

"Yes in Salonica."

There was instant relief on Rachelle's face as she didn't enjoy Lola's fateful reading.

"Am I going to have children?" she asked.

"I see a pregnancy," replied the gypsy.

"Can you tell me how many children I will have, because I want to have many."

The gypsy fell silent as she turned pale.

"That's all I can see for now," said the gypsy abruptly ending the reading, "Come back next year. I'll be here."

The two cousins stood up and walked away, sceptical of what they had just been told. That evening at home Lola told her father what had occurred at the fair and she made a point of how the gypsy turned extremely pale during Rachelle's reading.

"I believe she saw something bad but she didn't tell her what it was," said Lola.

"Sometimes gypsies are accurate and sometimes they couldn't be more wrong," replied Lola's father, "Trust me my daughter, don't give it a second thought."

And with that Lola never thought of the gypsy's reading again until Birkenau when she could see her cousin Rachelle wasting away before her eyes. Each week during *blocksperre,* Lola's heart would skip a beat, hoping that her cousin passed the inspection and that her pregnancy was not visible. If the SS doctors suspected a pregnancy, she would immediately be sent to the gas chambers or to Doctor Mengele for cruel experimentation. In Auschwitz-Birkenau, pregnant women were not spared as there was no use for them.

One evening after having come back from a hard day's work, Rachelle complained of severe stomach cramps. She fell to the ground and without warning blood gushed from her as she lay there moaning. Lola together with a girl from Berlin carried her as quickly as they could to the hospital. As soon as they entered, a female Jewish doctor, herself a prisoner, approached them.

"I don't have any more room for a *muselmann*[104]," she said in German.

"I think she is having a miscarriage," replied the girl from Berlin.

The doctor ushered them through and pointed to a bed in what seemed like a surgical room. The girls left Rachelle in the care of the doctor and on their way to the barrack the Berlin girl attempted to explain to Lola, in sign language what the doctor had told her. She held up her two fingers and said, "*Ubermorgen*[105]."

After a while Lola understood that in two days she was to go back to the hospital to inquire about her cousin. The wait was unbearable for Lola as she worried about her cousin. Is she going to be alright? Did she lose a lot of blood? How long will she be there for? All these questions filled Lola's mind and all she could do was simply wait. Two days later, when Lola

---

[104] *German* A slang term used among captives of Nazi Concentration Camps to refer to those suffering from a combination of starvation and exhaustion.

[105] *German* In two days or day after tomorrow.

returned from a long day of hard labour, she found Rachelle lying on the bunk.

"I was going to come and visit you," she said, "I'm so glad you're back." Rachelle just lay there staring vacantly in front of her. All Lola could do was to stay with her and offer her whatever moral support she could, and pray desperately that Rachelle would be back on her feet as soon as possible. This did not eventuate and Rachelle even refused to go to work. She would have enough energy for *appell* but after that she would go back to her bunk as if she had given up. For the next two days, while at work, Lola's mind was on her cousin and whether or not she would still be alive upon her return to the barrack. On the third day, when Lola came back from work, she was shocked to find that Rachelle's bunk was empty. She approached the girl from Berlin and pointed towards her cousin's bunk. The girl touched Lola's shoulders and gently pushed her to sit on a bunk. She motioned in sign language that she would be back. A few minutes later, she returned looking very upset. Lola gazed up at her and said, "Crematoria?" The German girl nodded.

Lola began to sob, and the kind girl from Berlin sat next to her and in silence, they hugged each other. Deep down Lola knew that those who were unable to go to work, were rounded up and sent to the gas chambers three times a week as the barracks were raided during the day. And despite knowing that this was inevitable, she somehow wanted to believe in a miracle. Rachelle's death left an indelible scar on Lola. After all, she had been a bridesmaid at her wedding.

Throughout her life after the war, Lola frequently thought of her cousin and her husband, Iakov Trapero. She never did find out what had happened to him nor did she ever hear of him again.

Chapter Four

(iv) Father and Moishe

As the weeks went by, appell wasn't as torturous due to the improved weather. Lola had heard from the other girls that July had arrived. During the day it was sunny but not hot like back home. Here in this foreign land the heat was bearable. On these warmer days, when they arrived back from work, many of the girls chose to spend whatever daylight was left, sitting together outside the barrack. They had been advised by the veterans to spend as much time outdoors as possible because when winter arrived, everyone would choose to be confined to the barracks because of the freezing weather.

On one of these sunny afternoons Lola was approached by Daphne, a new arrival from Salonica.

"Lola, your father wants to see you." She said urgently.

Daphne had seen Lola's father in a group of men digging behind the barrack when she was on her way to empty a latrine bucket.

"My father?"

"Yes, one of the men standing in line outside our barrack asked me if I know of a girl called Lola, he told me he's your father."

Lola took some time to process what she had just heard. She believed that her father was gassed upon arrival three months earlier.

"Are you sure he asked for me?"

"Yes. He said for you to be careful. When you go outside don't talk to him because the soldiers will shoot you. Just walk by him, he wants to see you."

"But how did you talk to him?"

"The soldier wasn't there, but now he's come back."

Lola stood up and ran, falling twice before she was even outside of the barrack. She then slowly walked past all the men who were working there, when suddenly her eyes met her father's. He smiled at her as tears rolled down his face. Lola smiled back and then started to cry. She stood there staring at her father. Daphne motioned to her to keep walking. There were SS Officers standing around with their huge German shepherds. Lola didn't want to arouse suspicion so she continued walking until she had encircled her barrack. Once she was back inside, she asked Daphne for a huge favour. There were certain times in Birkenau when there was no soup for the prisoners and instead they were given two potatoes each. Many of the girls held on to them so as to include them in their bowl when they were given soup.

"Please," said Lola, "Can you give me your two potatoes as I want to give them to my father together with my share? I will give you my new ration of potatoes tomorrow."

Daphne did not hesitate for a second. She pulled the potatoes out of her pocket and handed them to Lola. The only obstacle now was how to give the potatoes to her father. The men were working very close to where the latrines were emptied. Lola thought of a plan. She would take a bucket to be emptied and on her way back she would throw the potatoes near her father's feet. Lola and Daphne were carrying the bucket when suddenly one of the dogs began to bark. The German shepherd approached Lola pulling the SS guard who was holding its leash. The dog stopped right in front of her, barking and snarling as if it was ready to eat her alive. It was as though it had read her mind and knew of her secret plan. Lola just stood there as did Daphne, holding on to the bucket. She was so terrified at that moment, thinking that the guard was going to unleash the dog on her, but instead he pulled the dog away and began walking in the opposite direction. It took her a few seconds to get over her terror. Lola and her friend began walking and noticed that there were only two SS guards standing at least twenty metres away talking to each other. She knew this was her opportunity and Daphne was motioning to her to throw the potatoes towards her father. Lola then quickly bent down and threw the potatoes over to where her father was but they fell short. The four potatoes were picked up quickly by some of the starving men. Lola's father did not manage to get a potato but he smiled lovingly at his daughter acknowledging that it was the thought that counted. Lola had risked her life to give her father four small rotten potatoes. In the end it was that kind gesture that mattered. As Lola was about to leave, her father raised his hand in a fist shake, wanting to give her strength, to carry on, to not despair. She hurried back to the barrack with Daphne and as soon as they had put down the bucket, Lola began to sob uncontrollably. She could not believe that her father was alive. All she wanted to do was to kiss him and hug him. She wanted to talk to him, to tell him how much she loved him and how much she missed him. She knew that this was impossible and that her father would have been severely punished if she had. Lola remained on the ground there in front of the bucket as Daphne gently stroked her back.

That night, Lola lay sleepless on the bunk with four other girls leaning against her. She thought of how her father was alive and for the time being that is all she needed to know in order to carry on.

One week later, Lola was still getting over the shock of discovering that her father was alive. Hannah, a youthful looking twenty-five year old woman from Krakow came running into the barrack towards Daphne. Since they both spoke French and German they usually acted as interpreters for the girls. Hannah was speaking animatedly to Daphne and at the same time pointing towards Lola.

Daphne waved to Lola to come closer. Hannah spoke in French as Daphne translated.

"She says that a man is outside and is saying your name over and over." Due to the language barrier amongst the prisoners they spoke in whatever way they could to communicate. Hannah claimed when a group of male prisoners stopped outside their barrack, one of them kept saying over and over again, the one word which he believed the girls would understand, "Lola."

Lola rushed outside. She noticed some men standing in a line. One of them was smiling at her and as she looked more closely, she recognised her brother. She could not believe her eyes. Her brother was alive too. She went as close to him as she could, trying not to attract the attention of the guards who had gathered at one end of the line.

"Lola, eat whatever they're giving you. Don't look if it's good or not, just eat it." said Moishe.

She nodded, smiling at him. Lola and her only brother were staring at each with tears running down their cheeks. A few minutes later, the line of men began moving again. As soon as Lola went inside her barrack Daphne approached her.

"Who was he?" she asked.

"It was my brother Moishe, my only brother."

"I'm happy for you," said Daphne.

"At first, I didn't recognise him. He has lost so much weight and his magnificent head of hair is gone. But at least he's alive and hopefully he's together with my father."

Lola and Daphne hugged each other and for the first time since her arrival at Birkenau, Lola produced a huge smile. For the next six weeks, Lola practically had a skip in her step. Although she was stuck in hell with no end in sight, she was somehow happy, knowing that her beloved father and brother were still alive. She was so overjoyed that she even dreamt of Salonica for the very first time since her incarceration. In the dream, Lola and her brother were on a fishing boat in Kalamaria. They were both happy, laughing and talking. Together they threw the net into the sea and together they pulled the net out of the sea and it was filled with fish. Lola realised that this dream was influenced by the many boat trips she had taken with her brother. One memory that kept coming back to her was from the summer of 1939. The family was at their summer home on the Kassandra coast. Moishe had just turned eighteen and Lola was thirteen. She was a tomboy at that age and whatever adventure her brother was up to she was always included. One July afternoon just as the family had lain down under the pine trees, Moishe came and pulled Lola's pigtail. Once she realised who it was she got up and followed him to the back of the house.

"What is it?" she asked.

"Do you want to go on an adventure in baba's boat?"

"As long as we don't get into trouble, I do," said Lola nodding her head. They both climbed in and Moishe began to row the boat as Lola sat back. They travelled from the west side of the Kassandra coast all the way to the east side. Once they had arrived, Moishe showed Lola many small caves that were all along the beach. The small caverns were mysterious to Lola and they filled her imagination with creative thoughts which she wrote about for the rest of the summer. It was a glorious afternoon that Lola would never forget.

For the following few weeks, amidst the horror of life in Birkenau, such memories sustained Lola as she dreamed about the future and being able to relive these moments again with her brother. The future, however, was difficult to imagine as death surrounded her. She was constantly having to find ways to be resilient and to stay alive. Now that she knew that her brother and father were alive, her will to survive was even stronger.

One night Lola had the same recurring dream about her brother and the boat. This time however, the dream changed course right at the end. As usual Lola and her brother threw the net into the sea but when they pulled it out, instead of fish the net held her brother's corpse. In this dream, her father was with her in the boat. Once her brother's corpse was pulled onto the boat, her father disappeared and Lola was left all alone in the boat with her brother's dead body. Lola woke up in a sweat. To make matters worse, one of the four girls with whom she shared the bunk, had her elbow on Lola's chest and Lola found it hard to breathe. Suddenly she heard screams and realised that the truck had come and the women who were in the little room were going to be taken to the gas chamber.

The next day as Lola was dozing on her bunk after an exhausting days work, she was awoken by two familiar voices. Daphne was talking with a Greek man called Avram who often came to the women's barracks to repair whatever needed to be fixed. Lola knew Avram from Salonica and he always smiled at her whenever he came into their barrack. Lola immediately got up and approached the man. He had told her previously that he was in the same barrack as her father and brother.

"How are my father and brother?" she asked, "Do you still see them?"
Avram looked down and stopped what he was doing.
"Young lady, I don't have good news for you."
"What do you mean?"
"It's your brother…he's dead."
"He's dead? How?"

Avram did his best to explain to Lola what had happened to her brother. One morning following appell Moishe's number was called out. He stepped forward and was ordered to follow the SS Officer. That was the last time anyone saw him.

"Then how do you know he died?" asked Lola frantically.

"Because my brother-in-law is a Sonderkommando and he saw your brother shot and killed when he refused to do that job."

"He refused?"

Avram nodded.

"My brother would never refuse any job. I don't believe you."

"If you knew what kind of work your brother was asked to do, I think then you'd believe it."

As Lola stood there, in a state of shock, Avram hurriedly left the barrack as he had completed his work.

For the next few days, Lola was angry with her brother. All she could think of was her poor father who was left all alone to grieve his only son. Whatever was asked of her brother he should never have refused. These same resentful thoughts went over and over in her mind until one day she learnt all about the terrible work of the Sonderkommando. Her disappointment then turned into grief and pain. The misery and loss that Lola felt was indescribable. She now found herself mourning her brother for a second time. The thought of her father, alone and in pain, somehow kept her going.

Two months later in what was a chilly September, Avram came into the barrack to start up one of the two iron stoves that were installed there. It had been a while since she had heard anything about her father and once she saw that Avram was there, she approached him wanting to find out the latest news.

"Hello Mr. Avram," said Lola in Greek, "How is my father?"

The expression on Avram's face gave away the fact that he had been expecting this question. It was clear that he had prepared himself to break the tragic news to young Lola. Avram's thoughtful pause made Lola suspect the worst.

"Is my father dead?" she asked.

"Yes," replied Avram as he pretended to be preoccupied with repairing the iron stove.

"What happened?" asked Lola, who looked as though her world had come to an end.

Avram stopped working and took a look around the room to see if any guards were present. Once he saw that they were safe, he turned to Lola and explained gently what had occurred. Three weeks earlier, Lola's father had a bad case of diarrhoea for at least two days. Eventually he collapsed inside the barrack. He lay on the cold ground for many days. Nobody came to him. Nobody helped him.

"But why?" asked Lola.

"Your father had dysentery, which is why everyone kept away from him. No one wanted to catch it."

"And he died lying there like that?"

"Yes, he died a few days later."

Lola stood there for at least a minute longer as Avram continued to repair the iron stove. She then slowly turned around and walked back to her bunk. She lay on it and stared straight ahead. She did not sob or even cry, she just lay there, in complete silence.

"They have taken everything away from me," she muttered under her breath, "God, please take me with you, I am now ready to die."

In the morning, Lola awoke to the shouts of the female kapos. She was still alive. God had not answered her prayer, but somehow this did not surprise her anymore.

Chapter Four

(v) A Miracle

The autumn of 1943 was to become a most significant one for Lola. Her daily struggle for survival led to a shocking event that should have surely sent her to her death. Her circumstances could have secured her a place in the gas chambers, not once but five times. There were other victims who were sent to the crematoria for far less. But as it turned out, not for Lola. It was nothing short of a miracle that she remained alive.

Following the death of her father and brother Lola fell into a deep depression. She went about her daily routine in a daze, not caring about anything. She made no conscious attempt to stay alive. Lola had officially given up and she was now praying every night for God to take her. From a happy, bubbly person who loved life and wanted to live to her full potential, Lola had now become morose with her energy draining away day by day. Such a state of mind in Auschwitz-Birkenau usually had dire consequences.

One day in early October, Lola woke up feeling particularly lethargic. She even hesitated to go outside for appell but she had no choice. That day, the counting of the prisoners seemed to take forever and Lola already felt exhausted. All she wanted was a little bit of water. Suddenly Lola collapsed. She was still conscious but too exhausted to get up.

"Get up," whispered the girl next to her, "They will shoot you if they see that you're not standing."

This fell on deaf ears as Lola could not and would not stand up. Daphne, who was behind her, grabbed her and lifted her up.

"We're nearly finished here, hold on for a little while more," she said.

Lola wanted to collapse again but made every effort not to. At last the whistle blew and the women quickly dispersed. Lola was not hungry that morning. She just wanted to lie down.

"Come and get your coffee," said Daphne.

"I only want some water," said Lola.

"You can get some later," she said, "Come and get your coffee and piece of bread."

Lola wanted nothing but water.

The whistle sounded again and the female prisoners quickly lined up and began to make their way out of the camp where they went every day to dig aimlessly into the hard ground. As they marched along Daphne came up beside Lola.

"I will get you some water when we go back this evening."

Lola did not respond but this did not stop Daphne. She continued to talk to her and somehow give her encouragement.

That morning as usual, under the gaze of the SS guard, Lola dug into the ground with a pickaxe and tried to stay in exactly the same position, swinging the axe back and forth, with her feet planted firmly on the ground. She had previously discovered that by being in this same position for hours on end, she was able to keep standing as if something was holding her up. Despite it being autumn, the afternoon sun beat down onto the prisoners' heads. Although her head was covered with a striped kerchief, Lola's scalp felt like it was burning. She felt completely exhausted, but most of all she felt extremely thirsty. She glanced around and she caught sight of a bucket of water a little bit further up. Lola wanted nothing more than to have a drink from the bucket. In the back of her mind, she was aware that she could be shot for doing this but she did not care anymore. She calmly laid the axe on the ground and slowly made her way to the bucket of water. All she could think of was drinking some water. That's all she wanted. Nothing else. She reached the bucket and fell to her knees and in desperation, began drinking with her hands. The SS guard fired shots into the air but Lola ignored them. All she wanted was to drink the water.

Lola felt something nudge her on her left shoulder. She glanced down and saw a bullet fall next to her. She realised that she had been shot because she could see blood dripping onto the ground. The bullet had gone through her left shoulder. She sat down next to the bucket, bleeding and in shock. The SS guard made his way to where she was sitting and told her that she knew she was forbidden to drink. He walked away and Lola became enraged, wanting to strangle him. She wanted to stand up and tell him, "Listen you coward, if you want to kill me, go ahead and shoot me in the heart, but before I die I will have as much water as I want."

Something stopped her from following her impulse. Instead, with a bleeding shoulder, she remained seated next to the bucket of water for the rest of the day. She felt no pain, nor could she feel her shoulder. In a strange way she felt somehow relieved because she was not on her feet and she had quenched her thirst. Lola dozed off for what seemed like a moment before being woken up by the sound of the guard's whistle. Daphne quickly came up to her and helped her to stand.

"Come on! Let's go back to the camp," she said.

"Will they let me?" asked Lola.

She knew full well that anyone who was wounded at work for whatever reason would be taken to the little room behind the barrack to wait to be picked up in the middle of the night and taken to the crematorium.

"We'll see," said Daphne, "Just stay close to me and you must walk on your own."

Thirty minutes later they had arrived at the camp. Lola was expecting to be ushered away by the SS guard. As they got closer to the barrack, the guard who had shot her approached her and signalled for her to go inside her barrack. Once inside, Daphne and three other girls surrounded Lola and told her to sit on her bed and not move.

"You are so lucky," said Daphne, "I can't believe he didn't send you to the crematorium."

Lola was silent. She knew she had been chosen to live but she didn't know for how long. At the far end of Lola's barrack there was a small room that contained medical supplies to tend to scratches and sores. One of the girls in the barrack had a sister who worked in the hospital so they always had refills.

"Lola, we are going to pour antiseptic on your wound. Brace yourself because it's going to hurt," said one of the girls.

Daphne held on to her hand and squeezed it tightly. As they poured the antiseptic Lola began to scream. One of the girls quickly shoved a cloth into Lola's mouth. To Lola it felt like hot olive oil was being poured on her. They placed a piece of gauze on the wound and helped her to lie down on her right side. For the rest of the evening Lola lay there in pain. Her shoulder felt boiling hot and the pain was excruciating. That night the girls who usually shared the bunk with Lola went elsewhere but Daphne came and lay next to her.

"You'll be fine," said Daphne, "The antiseptic should prevent an infection."

"But I don't feel well," said Lola, "Before the antiseptic I wasn't in any pain, now I'm in constant pain."

"You don't want to get an infection," said Daphne, "That will be the end of you."

As Lola lay there sleeplessly, her mother's face appeared before her. But Lola was not happy, nor did it give her courage to go on. In fact, she felt quite the opposite. She was so angry with her mother. She had never felt this way before.

"Why?" she muttered under her breath. "Why did you bring me into this world?"

She kept repeating this over and over but there was no response. Lola knew that her mother was already dead, but her anger towards her still continued.

Eventually, Lola drifted off to sleep and when she awoke in the morning, she was burning up and her forehead was wet with sweat.

"Come Lola," said Daphne, "You must come to appell."

Lola lay there in silence, sweating and trembling all over. She was unable to get out of the bed let alone to go out of the barrack. She fell in and out of consciousness as the other prisoners stood outside during roll call.

When it was over, Lola saw the black boots of the SS guard approach her bunk. She recognised his voice. It was the same guard who had shot her.

"Take her to the hospital," he ordered.

"Come on Lola," said Daphne, "You've been given permission to go to the hospital."

With great difficulty Lola stood up with the help of Daphne and they walked slowly to the hospital which was half a kilometre away. When they arrived at the hospital, Daphne explained that Lola had permission from the SS guard to be there. There was a female Jewish doctor from Estonia who immediately set up a bed for Lola. This was the second time that Lola had been chosen to live. Very rarely, if ever, would a prisoner be allowed to live if they had failed to attend appell.

The following three days were touch and go for Lola. She was constantly falling in and out of consciousness. Her entire body was burning up, and the truth is there wasn't much they could do. There were no antibiotics to give her. All they could do was to continue cleaning the wound and place antiseptic lotion on it. They also gave her a cup of water every hour and wiped the sweat off her face. The doctor allowed her to sleep all day and all night.

On the fourth day, Lola's fever broke and for the first time she was able to sit up. In the evening when Daphne came to see her, the same doctor, whose name Lola did not know and never learnt, came and sat by her bedside. She spoke in French with Daphne as the interpreter.

"I don't want you to go back to the barrack yet because you are still very weak," she said, "We will give you soup to eat with a piece of bread twice a day. Try to eat it, it will do you good."

Lola nodded.

"Also there's one more thing," said the doctor, "Whenever an SS guard comes in here, keep your eyes closed and pretend to be very sick, because if you don't he will send you back to the barrack."

"Am I safe here?" asked Lola looking up at Daphne, "Because if I stay too long, won't they send me to the crematorium?"

"Don't worry," said the doctor, "You're safe here."

It wasn't until a few months later that Lola learnt from Daphne that the Estonian doctor was manipulating the paper work. In cases like Lola's when the person was young, strong and had potential to survive Auschwitz-Birkenau, the doctor did whatever she could to keep the patient from being sent to the gas chambers. This was the third time that Lola had been chosen to live.

Lola spent three weeks in the hospital. Even though she hadn't completely recovered, she was fit enough to go back to the barrack. Her left shoulder still hurt, so when she was at work digging every day, she tried her best to keep the pressure off her left shoulder.

Despite these complications, Lola's biggest challenge came when she had to face the weekly inspections. Her wound had still not healed completely and it was obvious as Lola stood naked in front of the SS doctors. The first time she faced them after her return from hospital was the most difficult one as an SS doctors came over and stared at the wound. Lola's heart pounded heavily as she held her breath not knowing if she would be chosen to live or die. In her state of fear, Lola did something completely unexpected. She took the doctor's right hand and kissed it, the way her friends in Salonica would kiss a priest's hand. She did not know what came over her. She was just desperate and did not want to be gassed; she didn't want to die that way. The SS doctor did not pull his hand away, instead he stared at her for a few seconds before motioning for her to go and put her clothes back on. She was not going to go through the selection. For the next three months this same SS doctor excused her from going through the selection. It was the fourth situation that Lola had been chosen to live.

During these months, despite her luck, the other girls did not hate her. Instead they looked upon her like someone who had special powers. During a selection, the number of an eighteen year old girl from Lublin had been recorded by one of the SS doctors. This girl's sister, Rosa, approached Lola and asked her if she could use her influence to save her little sister. Lola told her that the SS doctor who favoured her had already gone. If she was to approach any other SS Officer she'd probably be shot. Rosa then fell to the ground and began to sob. She did not want to go on living without her baby sister. She had already lost her entire family.

Lola's heart sank. She told her that she would try to do what she could.

"Lola where are you going?" asked Daphne.

"I have to do something," she said.

"No you don't," said Daphne, "If you approach an SS Officer and make a request, he will shoot you immediately."

"But I have to," said Lola, "I feel guilty for having being spared from the weekly selections."

"We all have our good luck and bad luck in this place. Don't throw your luck away."

"If I die, I die," said Lola She then turned and walked towards the wooden door.

Once she was outside, she saw two SS Officers with two big dogs, standing in front of the barrack. They turned and looked at her as though she was crazy. In half-broken German that she had already learnt in the camp, she explained that her little sister's number had been recorded and that she didn't want her to die. One of the SS Officers asked for her sister's number.

"42864", replied Lola.

The Officer nodded and Lola turned around and began to walk back, convinced that she would be shot at any moment. As soon as she entered the barrack, all the women were on their feet, clapping. Rosa embraced her and they both cried as they hugged each other. Lola felt that this was the fifth time that she had escaped death. A few hours later, when the numbers were called out, Rosa's sister's number wasn't among them. Lola, more than anyone, could not believe that her plan had worked. Soon after Lola was transferred elsewhere in the camp and she did not see the sisters from Lublin ever again.

[Fifteen years after her arrival in Australia, she came across a fellow prisoner of the same barrack. She told Lola that she was the bravest person she had ever known. She also told her that Rosa and her little sister survived the war and were smuggled into Palestine in 1946.]

Lola's luck was something that she never quite understood. She often wondered if it was a higher power that had miraculously helped her to survive the gunshot wound or if it was simply luck.

Chapter Five

Kanada

(i) *A New Job*

One year after Lola's arrival in Auschwitz-Birkenau, on a bitterly cold morning in mid-March, Lola and all the women of her barrack were getting ready to parade in front of the doctors. Unbeknownst to Lola this was to be the last medical selection she would have to go through at Auschwitz-Birkenau. As usual, Lola undressed completely and as she filed past the doctor sitting behind the desk, he motioned for her to hurry by. Once again she had passed the test. After the selections, the whistle blew for all of them to line up. A male SS Officer whom Lola had never seen before, approached them with the doctor who was often at the weekly selections. They stood in front of the women and the SS doctor began to point at some of them, slowly and methodically. The chosen ones came forward and stood on the side. Both Lola and Daphne were amongst those selected. Once this process had been completed, a female SS Officer motioned for the girls to follow the male Officer. They had no idea where he was leading them. Expecting to exit the camp, Lola was surprised to discover that they were being taken somewhere else inside the camp. They soon arrived in front of some huge wooden warehouses. Lola and Daphne were assigned to the same warehouse. As they entered they saw massive piles of suitcases, clothing and other items. They were instructed by a kapo woman to wear white kerchiefs on their heads.

They were told to sit at a table and were shown what to do by another prisoner. They learnt where to place each item from the suitcases. The men's pants, shirts and jackets went into three huge wooden containers. The women's clothes were also separated. The dresses and skirts were placed in the same container and the blouses and jackets in another. The children's clothing went into yet another container. That first day at Lola's new job seemed overwhelming but also strangely unreal. It took her a while just to finish two suitcases and once she was done, two more suitcases were brought to her. Lola gazed up for a moment and noticed the kapo woman who smiled at her. Lola smiled back. She was a bit bewildered because the kapo women in her last location did not smile.

Lola hoped and prayed that at this job, there would be less violence, brutality and dehumanization. As that thought crossed her mind, she heard the most horrendous screams. They seemed to be coming from the women in the building next door. She gazed cautiously around the room and for a split second her eyes met Daphne's. They both quickly looked down again, not wanting to get into trouble as it was their first day. That evening after devouring the soup which for the first time had some pieces of potato in it, she began to chew hungrily on the piece of bread they had been given with their soup.
"Don't chew so fast," said Daphne, "Keep some for later on."
"I have kept the second piece of bread, which I will have in a few hours when I'm hungry again."

"I can't believe it," said Daphne, "We've been given two pieces of bread and the soup wasn't just dirty water."

"If it's going to be like this, we'll be fine," said Lola. "Hopefully the screaming that we heard today, we won't hear again."

"I think we will hear the screaming," said Daphne.

"What do you mean?"

"The Czech woman told me that we'll be getting extra pieces of bread and we won't have to worry about working outdoors anymore. However, the downside is that we'll have to put up with the people's screams."

"I know that they were being killed but why didn't the bullets kill them instantly?" asked Lola.

Daphne stared at her and despite all of the horrendous things that Lola had witnessed in Auschwitz-Birkenau, there was still this naivety about her.

"They weren't shot," said Daphne, "Did you hear any gunfire?"

"No," said Lola, "But what was it that made them scream?"

"It was the gas," replied Daphne, "They were screaming because they were suffocating, knowing that soon they would be dead."

"Do you mean to tell me the gas chamber is next door?"

"Not exactly," said Daphne, "If you look out of the back window just behind those boxes, you'll be able to see a wooden house. It's called crematorium IV and that's where they're gassed."

Lola stood up and walked over to the back window. She gazed silently out of the window and when she returned to sit next to Daphne, she began to cry.

"I don't want to hear those screams again," she said as Daphne hugged her tightly.

"The Czech woman told me that we'll get used to the screams. She told me this is a much better place to be than where we were before."

"Who is this Czech woman?" asked Lola.

"Do you remember seeing a woman this morning who didn't have a shaved head?"

"Do you mean the woman with the beautiful dark hair?" asked Lola.

Daphne nodded.

"That's what my hair looked like before they shaved my head," said Lola. Despite it being on her mind, Lola never found out why the Czech woman had all her hair. Why her hair was not clipped would remain a mystery. It was not because her hair had grown back. Lola knew this because her hair had hardly grown in the year since it had been shaved.

"She is lucky," said Daphne, "Somehow she escaped the clippers."

That evening as Lola lay on her bunk, Daphne climbed up and sat next to her.

"I just found out something," she said.

"What?" asked Lola.

"They call this place *White Kanada*; do you know why?"

"No," replied Lola.

"Because of all the beautiful items that are in the suitcases."

"I only found clothes," said Lola.

"That was today," said Daphne, "But in the coming days, you're bound to find gold, money and even diamonds."

"But why do they call it *Kanada*?" asked Lola.

"Because of the country Kanada," replied Daphne.

Lola continued to stare at her.

"Haven't you heard about the riches of Kanada?" asked Daphne.

"No, I've only heard about the riches of America," she replied.

"That's where Kanada is," said Daphne, "It's in north America."

"But why *White Kanada*?" she asked.

"Because half of the warehouses are called *white Kanada* and the other half *red Kanada*. Our warehouse is in the section of *white Kanada*."

"Is that why we were given white kerchiefs to wear?" asked Lola.

"Yes," replied Daphne.

Lola's first day at *Kanada* was not only overwhelming but mentally exhausting as well. So much so that she didn't even realise and appreciate that she had an entire single bed to herself. There were twenty-six bunks at the back of the warehouse. For the next ten months Lola worked and slept in the same place with fifty other women. She and Daphne shared a bunk and she had the top bunk to herself with Daphne on the bottom bunk. Once again there were no mattresses, just straw. There were no blankets or pillows either.

The following morning, Lola realised that *appell* was not going to be a part of her daily schedule. As soon as they were woken in the morning, they would all use the latrines and the wash rooms. They were then given *ersatz* coffee just as before but with two slices of bread instead of one and every other day some margarine as well. As soon as they had finished their breakfast, a kapo woman would blow the whistle and all the women would start to work. Many times she sat there and could not believe her luck until she heard the wailing cries coming from the wooden house across the pathway.

One day, when the kapo and SS Officers were not present, Lola approached the window where the other girls were looking out. She saw a long line of men, women and children going past as the SS men stood by with their dogs talking and laughing. She turned and looked at Daphne.

"Are all these people going to be gassed?"

Daphne nodded.

Lola placed her hand over her mouth. She was horrified. She knew that they were unaware that they were going to their deaths but Lola knew and that's what made it unbearable. She saw young mothers, teenage girls, old men and the most beautiful children walking by and to make matters worse the children waved at the women who were looking at them from the warehouse windows. Lola felt as though her heart was being shredded into hundreds of tiny pieces.

This was the scene that could be witnessed from the small windows of the *Kanada* warehouses on a daily basis.

From their arrival at the camp to their death it could take as little as five hours to kill hundreds of innocent people at one time. They were told that they were going to have a shower and every piece of clothing must be removed. They were specifically told to remember the number of the peg where they hung their clothes so that they could quickly find their clothes after the shower. Once inside, the door of the gas chamber was bolted and the screams began. After ten minutes the screams began to fade and after twenty minutes all was quiet. Lola knew that they were all dead. Their bodies were then burnt in the crematorium ovens. Every day Lola waited for that terrible smell of burnt human flesh to waft through the warehouse. She had no choice but to sit there and to endure it.

One day a female SS Officer came to Lola's warehouse. The girls stood up and faced the Officer. She had something to say:
"We all know that the Jews have money, gold and diamonds. We also know that they are very clever in hiding their precious possessions, so that is why we will give you a demonstration of where to look for these items." The kapo woman standing next to the Officer began to tear open the lining of a woman's jacket all the way to the hem. This is what Lola had to do on a daily basis. Before placing the clothes in the appropriate boxes, she had to tear them apart. There were many times that she found diamonds, foreign currency and gold jewellery inside the lining of garments. When Lola first found uncut diamonds she thought they were pieces of glass and she began playing with them, as she had never seen diamonds in this state before.
"What are you doing?" asked Daphne as she caught Lola throwing the diamonds up.
"I'm playing *Jacks*," said Lola.
"With the diamonds?"
Lola then stopped and stared at Daphne.
"Are they diamonds?"

"Yes," said Daphne.

"I didn't know. I thought they were pieces of glass."

Daphne brought over two large suitcases which she placed next to Lola. She instructed her to place the diamonds in one suitcase and the jewellery in the other. She brought one more suitcase.

"In this suitcase, you will place the coins and paper money."

"Do I separate the different currencies?"

"No," replied Daphne, "You place it all in here."

The following afternoon after having sorted ten suitcases of children's clothes into the appropriate wooden boxes, the Czech woman told Lola that she had to tear every single piece apart because one of the other girls found gold jewellery in the lapel lining of a boy's jacket. After that day, they were ordered to tear apart the children's clothes as well.

"Where do they take all these things?" asked Lola that evening as she sat next to Daphne to eat her soup.

"To Germany," she replied.

"What about the money?"

"It's deposited into German banks."

"But this is theft. They are killing everybody and then they're stealing their belongings."

"If there is a God, they will be punished."

"But there's so much of it," gasped Lola, "And it continues to come."

"Now you know why this place is called Kanada," said Daphne.

"Yes I do," said Lola as she continued to eat her meagre meal.

Chapter Five

(ii) *Fury*

Lola's work in the Kanada warehouse allowed her much more time to think than she had experienced since her arrival at Auschwitz-Birkenau. All the thinking, however, was turning into anger. She knew she could never show her fury to her captors and this was especially difficult for her from the beginning of May with the arrival of the Hungarian Jews. Kanada had turned into bedlam with the influx of the victims' belongings, as the gas chambers began running on a 24-hour cycle. There were three gassings during the day, and two during the night and it remained like that until the beginning of September, when the gassing took place again only during the day. The screams that could be heard in the middle of the night woke up all the girls. After all, a pathway just 20 metres wide is what separated their warehouse from crematorium IV.

One morning in mid-May, six new girls were brought in from the women's barracks. They were to replace the girls that had been sent to red Kanada which was situated directly behind their warehouse. At this particular time, due to the arrival of Hungarian Jews, there was constant upheaval at Kanada.

The first thing that Lola noticed about the new girls was that they looked extremely thin and worn down. They were immediately put to work sorting out the victims' personal belongings. During that evening, as Lola rested on her bunk, she felt a nudge on her leg.

"Lola, get up," said Daphne, "I want to introduce to you Eutixia."

Lola was up in an instant as she recognized the Greek name.

The three girls felt an immediate bond and for the duration of the evening the new arrival told them of her ordeal. She was from the western Greek city of Ioannina. The Jews of that town were Romaniote[106] Jews whose roots dated back to antiquity. Until the end of March 1944, they were left alone by the Nazis. On the 25th of that month, on Greek Independence Day, they were rounded up, and as snow flurries fell, two thousand people were placed on open trucks and taken to a railway station 50 km away. Amidst terror, noise and madness they were loaded onto the cattle trains and did not get off until nine days later when they had arrived at Auschwitz.

"So how long have you been here for?" asked Lola.

"About a month," replied the shy delicate faced girl.

As their discussion progressed, Lola and Daphne were shocked to learn that Eutixia did not speak Ladino.

"I'm not Sephardic[107]," said the girl from Ioannina, "I'm a Romaniotissa."[108]

She explained to them that she spoke Yevanic[109], a two and a half thousand year old language, and that their traditions differed from those of the Sephardic Jews.

---

[106] The Romaniote Jews are a Jewish community who have lived in Greece for more than 2000 years.

[107] Descendants of the Jews who lived in Spain and Portugal during the Middle Ages until the 15th and 16th centuries.

[108] *Greek* A Romaniote-Jewish girl or woman.

"You're the first Jewish girl I have ever met to have the name Eutixia," said Lola.

Eutixia was a typical Greek Christian girl's name which the Sephardic Jews of Greece did not name their daughters.

"The fact that I'm named Eutixia shouldn't be that surprising to you because it means Mazel Tov."[110]

Lola and Daphne looked at each other. Here they were, stuck in the middle of hell, not knowing if they would live or die, and they were still learning new things about their people, even from the brink of destruction.

"Yes," said Eutixia, looking at the shocked expression on the girls' faces. "In Greek, my name means 'good luck' as does 'Mazel Tov' in Hebrew."

"You're right it does," said Daphne, "But it's something I had never thought about before."

Eutixia told them that evening how she found out in the women's camp about the gassing of her family. She began to sob uncontrollably. Lola and Daphne cried with her and hugged her in an attempt to console her.

The following morning it was time for their weekly shower. The central sauna house was located directly across from the Kanada warehouses. As the girls from Lola's block made their way there they saw a long line of women who were new arrivals. They had been selected to work and they were lined up outside the building waiting to enter in order to be

---

[109] A Greek dialect spoken by Romaniote-Jews. It is infused with Hebrew words and written with the Hebrew script.
[110] A Jewish phrase that means good luck and is used to express congratulations.

processed. As Lola and the other girls passed them she said to Eutixia, "This is where you were given your tattoo and the striped garment that you're wearing when you first arrived here."

Eutixia nodded and looked bewildered, not having fully familiarised herself with the camp's buildings. They entered that same building from a side door. The weekly showers were appreciated during the summer months but as soon as the cold weather began they dreaded them, as they did not know if the water would be cold or warm.

One evening as the women sat sipping their soup with their stale piece of bread, Daphne asked Eutixia if the screaming of the people had made her go crazy yet.

"No," she replied, "I don't think it ever will, because for me I prefer to hear screams than seeing dead bodies lying around and then being forced to pick them up like dead animals and pile them up one on top of the other in the corner. This is what nearly made me crazy in the other barrack."

The next few weeks seemed to pass by without anything extraordinary happening. Then, one evening, as Lola sat quietly on her bunk, she heard loud male voices singing a familiar song in Greek.

Greece never dies,
She is not afraid of anyone,
She only relaxes for a short time,
And then again She leads to Glory.

That song was followed by a few seconds of silence. Suddenly another song started up, which she instantly recognised as the Greek National Anthem.

I recognize you
From the sword's fierce blade,
I recognize you
From the guise of your face
Counting the lands restored, in haste.

You have emerged
From the sacred bones of Greeks,
And just as brave as before,
Hail, oh hail, Liberty!

Half way through the anthem, she heard machine gun fire followed by complete silence. For the two months that Lola had been at Kanada, at least once a fortnight she had heard young men who had been forced to become *Sonderkommando* singing their country's national anthem before being gunned down by the SS. This was the first time that she had heard her own country's anthem. Lola saw Daphne and Eutixia go to the window. When the shooting had stopped they came over to her.
"We didn't see them," said Eutixia.

"That's because they shoot the *Sonderkommando* on the other side where there are no windows," said Daphne.

"That was *our* national anthem," said Lola.

"I hope there wasn't anyone I know," said Eutixia.

Daphne and Lola looked at each other, as they knew that it was highly likely that Eutixia knew some of the *Sonderkommando* who had just been shot. Daphne later told Lola in secret that the young men who sang the Greek National Anthem were most likely from Ioannina. She told her not to say anything to Eutixia so as not to traumatise her. It was also during this time that Lola and Daphne came to know a few of the Greek sonderkommando. Every now and again, always in the evening when the SS weren't around, one of the Greek sonderkommandos would come into their warehouse and ask the girls if they found any liquor or cigarettes amongst the belongings. Sometimes they would stay a while and talk with the Greek female prisoners. This is when Lola learnt that most of the Greek Sonderkommando worked in crematoria IV and V. Some of them were required to move the corpses from the gas chambers and others were given the task of placing the dead bodies in the furnaces.

On one of these occasions a Greek from Larissa whose name was Aleko approached Lola and asked if she had found any ouzo[111].

"No," she replied in Greek, "But I did find a camera, it's over there in that box."

The tall Greek man sifted through the box and picked up the camera. After examining it, he said, "It has a roll of film in it. I'm going to take it."

---

[111] A Greek aniseed-flavoured spirit.

"Take it, take it," said Lola.

During the next two months Lola and her friends heard their country's national anthem four more times, always followed by machine gun fire. Whenever this occurred Lola would wonder which of the Greek Sonderkommando who had become her friends, were amongst the victims. In late July, word spread amongst the Greek prisoners that the Jews of Corfu had arrived. Lola, Daphne and Eutixia prepared themselves to hear their national anthem, but for some unknown reason they never did.

By mid-August, the smell of the bodies had become overwhelming. One day, Lola stood at the window on the other side of the warehouse, hoping to get a reprieve from the smell. In order not to get into trouble she pretended to sort women's cosmetics that were piled up in a box. She removed the lipsticks and placed them in a smaller box. As she did this, she was staring out of the window and saw new arrivals walking past. She saw an old man in the group. He looked like an Orthodox Jew, not only because of his beard but also because of the fringe tassels of his prayer shawl that were visible beneath his shirt. As he went past two SS Officers, who were standing there with two German shepherds, talking and laughing, the old man removed his hat as a show of respect to the Germans. Lola's heart began to beat very quickly. She was overcome with rage.

"If you only knew where you were going," she muttered under her breath. She could not believe that there was such deception surrounding the murder of her people; that moments before they were murdered, they would continue to bow to their murderers.

During that same month, Lola was to discover that the Jews weren't the only ones being gassed. One day, when there were no guards and kapos around, Daphne motioned to both Lola and Eutixia to come to the window.

"Do you see these children with their mothers?" she asked, as a long line of innocent souls passed by.

"Yes," said Lola, "What about them?"

"The Czech woman told me that they're not Jews."

Lola and Eutixia turned and looked at Daphne.

"They're Russians…," said Daphne.

"Christians?" asked Lola.

Daphne nodded.

"Why are they here?" asked Eutixia.

"They're political prisoners."

"So they will be put to work," said Lola.

"Only the mothers, not the children."

Lola and Eutixia knew instantly what was going to happen to the children. Their warehouse was left unguarded that day was because the Nazis needed all the help they could get. They were expecting mayhem to erupt as the mothers would refuse to part from their children. What they had anticipated did happen. Within fifteen minutes of them passing by, unbearable screams were heard. Daphne, Eutixia and Lola watched as the SS guards pulled the children from the mothers and the female SS guards beat the mothers as they fell to the ground, trying to run after their children.

"I can't watch anymore," said Lola, as she went back to her place and resumed her work.

A few minutes later, the screaming had ceased and the children were swiftly gassed. That evening after getting the information from the Czech woman, Daphne told Lola and Eutixia that there had been a partisan attack on the German army about 100km from Leningrad. As a reprisal, the Nazis rounded up entire families from three villages. They shot the men and all boys over fifteen. Everyone else was deported to Auschwitz-Birkenau.

The following day as Eutixia was sorting out a pile of clothes, an icon of the Virgin Mary fell out of the pocket of a child's coat. She instantly recognized it as an Orthodox Christian relic since her own country had that religion and she knew that it probably belonged to a Russian child who was gassed the day before. She showed it to Daphne and Lola before placing it in the appropriate box that would eventually end up in Germany.

Chapter Five

(iii) Breaking bread with the enemy

As a girl from a traditional Jewish family, Lola was extremely familiar with the term *the breaking of bread*[112]. Her father would say this very often in Ladino or Greek. For the Jews, to break bread with someone was a very intimate act. Whether to have a meal with a friend or neighbour or when one wanted to show the act of forgiveness you invited the person to your home to break bread together. However, if one broke bread with the enemy, that was nothing short of treason. Lola knew this from a young age when she read the bible together with her father.

"It is better to face death than to break bread with the enemy," said Lola's father many times.

When Lola questioned the actions of some people in the bible breaking bread with the enemy, her father's response was always the same.

"If one breaks bread with a hostile enemy, who is hell-bent on destroying us, then he is either a traitor or a spy. There is no other explanation."

If Lola had learnt anything from her father, it was this truth.

For this reason, it was unbelievable and unacceptable to Lola that a fellow Jewish prisoner was breaking bread with the SS Officers.

"If she is breaking bread with them…"

---

[112] The origins of the expression date back to biblical times (Old Testament) when one tore pieces of bread from a loaf and shared it with others at a social gathering.

"Lola, what do you mean *if*, we all know she is," said Daphne angrily.

"Let me finish," said Lola, "If she is breaking bread with them, then she must be a spy."

Daphne and Eutixia stared at her in disbelief.

"Do you really think the Czech woman is a spy?" asked Eutixia.

"I don't believe that she's a traitor, because she is so nice to us," said Lola.

Daphne and Eutixia looked at each other.

Upon their arrival at Kanada, Lola and Daphne's first impression of the Czech woman was that she was beautiful with a full pile of hair, and the only prisoner to have pink, round cheeks.

It wasn't until later that Daphne began to be suspicious because of the Czech woman's absence during the evening and sometimes for the entire night. As days passed, Daphne, who spoke French, was able to communicate with some of the other women in Kanada and eventually pieces of information were divulged. It was said that she was having a sexual relationship with the SS guard Wunsch. Because of his obsession with the Czech woman he was at their warehouse practically every day. Needless to say, he was always courteous and nice to all the women. However, the female prisoners in Lola's block were divided about how they viewed the Czech woman. Some, like Daphne, were extremely polite with her but deep down resented her and saw her as the ultimate collaborator. Others were willing to put her cavorting with the enemy aside because she was kind to all the women. There were many times when she would return in the morning after being absent all night, with two loaves of bread and plenty of cheese, which she always shared with everyone there.

Despite the Czech woman never being a kapo, she was definitely the one who was in charge. When a kapo needed to be replaced she would find the replacement. One day in mid-June she approached Lola as she sat in her chair sorting out clothes. She asked her if she wanted to be a kapo. According to the Czech woman, all that Lola would be required to do was to see that everyone was doing their job, and to make sure no one slows down. Lola looked directly into the Czech woman's eyes.

"I can never be a kapo," she said. "A kapo needs to be strong and sometimes has to hit the others to do their job right. I cannot treat my people in this way, so choose somebody else."

That evening as Lola was having her soup and bread she saw Daphne walking towards her wearing the distinct kapo armband on her left arm. It was a piece of black material with the word KAPO written in white. She stopped eating and looked up.

"I can't believe you took on that job," said Lola.

"Don't worry," said Daphne, "I will treat you well."

"I hope you treat all of us well."

Daphne sat next to Lola and began to eat her soup. For the rest of their time in Auschwitz-Birkenau, Daphne was considered a *good* kapo by all of the women in Lola's block.

A few weeks later, as Daphne was making her usual rounds, she found a piece of paper on the floor. After reading it, she immediately approached Lola and sat down next to her.

"Won't you get into trouble?" asked Lola.

"I'm a kapo now," replied Daphne, "Besides, the Czech woman and the guards are not here."

She then showed Lola the piece of paper. There was a drawing of a love heart with some writing that Lola could not understand.

"Is that in German?" asked Lola.

Daphne nodded and then began to translate.

You are the most beautiful woman in the world. I dream about you all the time. I am in love with you. Franz.

"I told you she was having an affair with him," said Daphne.

"Do you mean the Czech woman?"

Daphne rolled her eyes.

"Yes," she said, "Wunsch and the Czech woman."

"Tell me something I didn't already know," said Lola.

It would seem that it was a mutual love affair between Franz Wunsch and the Czech woman. In the coming months, Daphne was to find four more love letters. Once she had shown them to some of the girls she would put them back exactly where she found them.

One day, another SS guard who hung around in Lola's block brought Lola some soup with a piece of bread. As she looked up she saw the other female prisoners glaring at her. She contemplated whether or not to eat the soup but her hunger pains were so severe that she gave in to her cravings.

A little while later, Daphne came up to her, "Lola, do you know why he gave you the soup?"

"Because he knows I must be hungry."

Daphne sat down beside her and told her that the SS guard wanted sexual favours. Lola refused to acknowledge this as she continued to eat the soup. That evening Daphne once again approached her and was firm with her.

"If he brings you soup again, don't accept it. Because he'll insist on having something in return and I don't want you to get hurt."

The SS guard never gave Lola anything ever again.

Some time later, due to a quarrel with Wunsch, that particular guard was to leave Lola's block for good. It turns out that because he was from the Sudetenland[113], he spoke the Czech language fluently and many times he was seen by all the women talking animatedly with the Czech woman. One day, Wunsch, who had witnessed this on several occasions, approached him and accused him of flirting with his girlfriend. Lola saw Wunsch push the other SS guard violently until he fell to the ground. That was the last time that he was ever seen in Lola's block.

In mid-July of 1944, the crematoria were at their peak due to the Hungarian transports. Crematorium IV which was across from Lola's block was constantly working day and night. On one of these very busy days, the girl from Prague – as she was known to the others – came rushing in to Lola's block. She had spent the morning sorting out the victims' belongings that had been offloaded from the latest train. She went

---

[113] The native German-speaking regions within the borders of the current Czech Republic, were referred to as the Sudetenland during the Second World War.

directly to the Czech woman and told her something. The Czech woman immediately dropped what she was doing and left the block with her. Soon after, the Czech woman came back in, frantically searching for someone. It was Wunsch that she was looking for. He was standing near Lola looking at some of the goods that she was sorting. Although Lola did not speak German, she had learnt to understand certain words and phrases after a year and three months in Auschwitz-Birkenau. It was clear to her that the Czech woman was begging for Wunsch's assistance.

"Please you have to do something. My sister and her children have just arrived from Hungary. They are already in the crematorium. You must save them."

"I can't save the children, they won't let me, but I *can* save your sister," he said.

Wunsch immediately left the block. He returned a short time later with the Czech woman's sister. The sisters embraced and began to cry. It wasn't until late that evening that the sister discovered the fate of her children. Tragically, the children had been immediately gassed with all the others in that transport. She began to hit the Czech woman violently with her fists and screamed out loud, "If you couldn't save my children you shouldn't have saved me. How do you expect me to go on without my children? You selfish bitch! I hate you! I hate you!"

Lola remembers that the woman was in her own black world surrounded by darkness. All she did was lie down all day and stare vacantly into the abyss. Her sister's negative demeanour did not seem to affect the Czech woman, and she continued on her merry way, smiling, sharing her food with the other women and being ever so grateful that her sister had been saved.

One evening, as Lola rested on her bunk, she noticed the Czech woman pass by and smile. When Lola smiled back, the woman climbed up onto the bunk and sat with her. Lola could tell that she was feeling lonely. In broken German Lola asked about her sister who was still in a state of shock. The Czech woman gave a timid smile and the look on her face said it all. Lola asked her where Wunsch was. The Czech woman explained to Lola that he had gone out with his fellow SS Officers. Lola admired her honesty. She had so much power that she could have you eliminated on a whim if she wanted to but she wasn't that type. She was a kind, caring person and despite the fact that she fraternised with the enemy, Lola could not hate her.

They sat in silence for a few more minutes before Lola spoke.

"Wunsch loves you very much," she said.

"I love him too," said the Czech woman, "And when the war is over I shall not see him again."

The Czech woman began to speak animatedly about her relationship with Wunsch. She told Lola that this was true love but she refused to go to Austria with him after the war. Wunsch had told her to follow him to Austria and they could marry. He really wanted that to happen but the Czech woman's loyalty was to her people. Having been a prisoner at Auschwitz-Birkenau, the Czech woman saw firsthand the murder of her people day in and day out. She had told Wunsch many times that after the war she will take her sister and go to Palestine. She felt she had a duty toward her people to try to help rebuild their Jewish homeland.

"How will you go there?" asked Lola.

"Where there's a will there's a way," replied the Czech woman.

Chapter Five

(iv) *The Revolt*

In early October, autumn had truly arrived. In Lola's block, all the girls felt it was colder than usual. Lola was very grateful that she was indoors all day.

She did not think about the future, even though rumours had begun to surface that the Russians were approaching fast. She had no way of knowing if she would survive and strangely enough, she didn't know if she wanted to. Her mother and father had been murdered, as had three of her siblings and both of her beloved grandmothers. Lola did not know if she could continue to live with the pain of that loss.

One day, as the girls were hard at work in the block, they heard a commotion outside. The SS were shouting and the girls could hear gunfire as well.

"Girls, don't move," said Daphne who came running in, "The *sonderkommando* are fighting with the SS guards."

Lola and the other women did their best to remain calm. They didn't know what was going on, all they could hear was shouts, gun shots and chaos. Suddenly, a massive explosion shook the entire place. The girls began screaming. Lola ran to cower on her bunk, as did the other women. Daphne who was still the kapo in charge did not stop them. Then the Czech woman entered the block looking extremely pale.

"Look at her," said Daphne to Lola and Eutixia, "She's concerned for her boyfriend. If I could kill her, I would right now."

"Don't be stupid," said Eutixia.

"I said 'if' I could! Obviously I can't."

"What exactly is going on?" asked Lola.

"There's been a revolt against these monsters, that's all I know." replied Daphne.

The fighting continued for a few more hours but the girls were told to get back to work. Lola tried not to think of what was going on outside. She concentrated on what was in front of her. She had found a photograph of three small children in the pocket of a woman's jacket. She continued staring at it intently. She was terrified that this could be her last day on earth. Lola was well aware of what the SS did to exact revenge, and she wouldn't be one bit surprised if they were to decide to shoot all the women in white and red Kanada. She continued holding the photograph in her hand and her focus was on the little boy's sailor suit outfit.

By night fall all had quietened down. As Lola sat eating her soup, Daphne came to tell her and the other girls the extraordinary news.

"I don't believe it," said Eutixia, "Do you mean it's completely destroyed?"

"Yes," replied Daphne, "Crematorium IV was blown up. It is officially out of commission."

"That's why the explosion was so deafening," said Lola.

As the evening progressed, Daphne, who had the authority to go in and out of the block, would return every half hour with news.

"How did they manage to get the explosives?" asked Eutixia.

Daphne leant forward as she sat on Eutixia's bed and whispered, "Apparently there was some kind of an underground resistance."

"Here, in Birkenau?" asked Lola.

"Yes," she replied, "But they only managed to blow up crematorium IV. The other three crematoria are still in use."

Lola and Eutixia could not believe that against all odds, the sonderkommando were able to stage the revolt and blow up crematorium IV. They paid a heavy price for their bravery as hundreds of sonderkommando were immediately murdered by the SS.

"This is a victory, no matter which way you look at it," said Eutixia, "Because one thing's for sure, there is one less gas chamber in this hell of a place. For that alone, they are heroes."

By the following morning the commotion seemed to have died down. Overnight there had been shootings and according to the rumours that were circulating, there was to be a crackdown on all the perpetrators. Lola and the girls in her block continued to work. By noon Lola realised something - she had heard no screams.

"If only they had blown it up earlier." she thought to herself.

For the first time in a long time, her nerves felt calm. She knew that she would not be hearing the screams any time soon. For the next few days, Daphne was filling them in on what was happening. She had found out from the Czech woman that Wunsch had not been injured at all, although he took part in quashing the revolt. The last time he had been in their block was the day before the uprising. He didn't come in again until mid-November.

A week later, Daphne had learnt an important piece of news.

"What have you learnt?" asked Lola as Daphne stood next to her.

"The SS have arrested one of the women in the next block."

"Who?" asked Lola.

"I don't know her name but she was somehow involved in the revolt."

As the weeks went by, it was evident that crematorium IV was not going to be rebuilt. Daphne made sure to keep them informed of any new developments. Eventually all the gas chambers ceased operating and the SS themselves began to blow up the crematoria, one by one. It seemed that many of the SS were frightened for their lives, especially with the Russians moving closer and closer. As the madness was slowly dying down, the will to survive amongst the female prisoners of Kanada was stronger than ever before.

Chapter Six

Ravensbruck

(i) *A Journey of Suffering*

In mid-January of 1945, rumours of the Russians nearing the camp became stronger. Lola and the other women in her block continued to do their jobs as usual without giving away what they had learnt secretly. The transports had ceased to arrive three months prior to this and in turn the gassings had stopped. However, the victims' belongings were still being sorted out, and there were still warehouses full of stolen goods and clothes. There wasn't a day that Daphne did not hear something on the grapevine. She would immediately tell the girls in her block of uplifting news.
"It's nearly over. The Russians are within miles," she would whisper to each woman individually.
Every time Daphne had news, Lola would pray silently, "Please God, lead the Russians to us."
She prayed and hoped like never before until once more her hopes were completely shattered. One frightfully cold January morning, after Lola had eaten her stale piece of bread, she returned to her chair and began to unload the clothes from a suitcase. As always, whenever she had a brand

new suitcase to unload she would always look to see the name on it. This one was labelled:

Regina Hoffmann,

Budapest, Hungary

Like always she would try to work out the age of the person by the contents of the case. The first item she pulled out was a book on ancient Rome. It was in a foreign language which she assumed was Hungarian. Then she found a light blue shirt very similar to one that she had at home in Salonica. She instantly knew that the owner of the suitcase was most likely a girl her own age. This turned out to be the last suitcase that Lola unpacked and therefore she always remembered the name written on it. Suddenly, the SS female guards came into the block and began to yell, "Raus, raus[114]."

All the girls ran outside and were exposed to the freezing cold wind that they were not used to. Daphne came around and gave each girl a blanket.

"What's happening?" asked Lola.

"We're leaving the camp."

"Where are we going?"

"God only knows," replied Daphne.

Lola covered her head and body with the blanket and to the sound of a whistle they all began to walk off in a straggly line. They walked along a road, passing through villages, past houses and occasionally encountering passers-by who would not look at them. The minutes turned into hours without any end in sight. As Lola trudged along trembling from the cold,

---

[114] *German* Get out

an SS woman came around handing out extra blankets, which Lola immediately accepted. Lola suddenly felt very angry. She could not believe that for two years they didn't even have a blanket to cover themselves at night and now miraculously they even had spare ones. At one stage as they were ordered to stop. Lola looked behind her and saw a sea of people. She knew then that the entire camp was being evacuated. Lola had lost track of time. She was so in her own world that she didn't realize the sun had set until the SS guards led them into a huge barn where they sat wherever they could. Lola, Eutixia and Daphne huddled up together. They were hungry and exhausted. They were given a piece of bread and nothing else. They ate it with gratitude.

"I want some water," said Eutixia.

"I want some hot tea," said Lola.

"I'm really thirsty," said Eutixia as Daphne and Lola looked at her.

She looked pale and although all the girls were completely worn out, Eutixia looked very sick. Daphne wanted to help Eutixia. She looked around for the Czech woman and suddenly realised that she wasn't there.

"I don't think she came with us," said Lola.

"I think you're right," said Daphne, "I bet her SS boyfriend warned her of the evacuation."

Suddenly, Eutixia fell back and closed her eyes.

"Let her sleep," said Daphne, "I will try to fetch some water for her."

Since the Czech woman was not there, Daphne had no choice but to ask for some water from the female SS guard who was often on duty at Kanada.

Lola watched nervously as Daphne approached the guard. The guard went outside with her and a few minutes later Daphne returned with a cup of water. Lola and Daphne did not take one sip, although that's all they wanted to do. They guarded the cup of water carefully, making sure they did not spill a drop and ensuring it did not get stolen. At daybreak, Lola was woken by the sound of a rooster crowing. She had not heard that sound for years. She looked over at Eutixia who was awake. She helped her with some water and the rest she shared with Daphne.

After receiving a piece of bread each, they were all ordered to get up and start moving. It was their second day on the road. As Eutixia began to stumble, Lola and Daphne placed her in between them and held her arms on either side. They told her to sleep if she has to. Eutixia sleepwalked for nearly the entire day. As that day progressed Lola and Daphne began hearing shots. They had been warned before leaving Auschwitz-Birkenau that if you could not continue the journey, you would be shot. After a while they lost count of the gunshots and were more determined than ever to hold onto Eutixia. By nightfall they had reached a barbed wire fence and they entered another camp. They were taken to some barracks that were already packed full of female prisoners from other camps.

The only place to sit or lie down was the cold wooden floor. There they fell asleep exhausted and extremely hungry. After what seemed like a very short sleep, they were woken by the SS guards who yelled at them to stand up and start walking. Lola and Daphne helped Eutixia up and just like before they held her from either side. As they left the barrack, Lola realised that it was still the middle of the night. A fellow female prisoner whom Lola had never seen before gave each woman a loaf of bread. Daphne asked her, "Do you know where we are?"

"Gleiwitz," she replied before moving on.

Lola stared at the loaf of bread. She was happy and sad. For the first time in two years she had an entire loaf of bread to herself but she was also certain that a long, horrendous march awaited them. They walked out of the camp, but before long they were ordered to stop. A convoy of open freight train cars came past them and stopped. There was pushing and shouting as the SS guards loaded them onto the train.

"Macht schnell, macht schnell,"[115] they screamed.

Daphne was the first to get on to one of the freight cars and she then helped Eutixia, Lola and all the others until it was fully occupied.

Lola and Eutixia were sitting together in the corner of the freight car and Daphne sat down directly opposite them.

The open freight car began to move. Lola was relieved that at least wherever they were headed they didn't have to walk but they were exposed to the elements as there was no roof over their heads. Lola tried to be positive by staring at the two loaves of bread on her lap. Eutixia had instantly fallen asleep and had her head resting on Lola's shoulder. Lola tried to break the bread with her hand but was unable to. She realized how weak she was. She held the bread to her mouth and chewed it very slowly until she had gone through the crust. Lola was so exhausted that she slept but had no idea how long for.

---

[115] *German* Hurry up.

Lola was experiencing bad stomach pains and she had no choice but to relieve herself where she sat. Occasionally she would look over at Eutixia and was envious of her as she continued to sleep.

Lola became so thirsty that she felt she would pass out. It began to snow heavily and Lola opened her mouth wide in order to catch the snow. When her loaf of bread was covered in snow, she would lick it all off. For two days straight all she remembers was eating the snow that fell down into their train car.

Sometimes, the train would come to a complete halt. On three of these stops, the SS came around ordering everyone to throw the corpses out of the cars. So many people were dying that the freight cars were now a lot less crowded. Eventually, Daphne was able to sit next to Lola. She looked over at Eutixia and reached over to touch her face. She turned to Lola and said, "I think she's gone."

"But she can't be gone," said Lola, "She's been sleeping the whole time."

"She's as white as a sheet, and as frozen as an ice block. I'm telling you she is gone."

Lola knew that it was true. She just did not have the strength to cry or even to mourn her dear friend. She knew that she could very well be the next corpse on that wagon. On the third stop, Daphne and Lola picked up the lifeless body of their friend and threw her off the train. As they sat down, Lola felt a deep sense of sorrow, not only for herself but for the entire world. The cruelty and the despicable events that she was constantly forced to endure were never ending. She sat there and wept whilst Daphne said Kaddish[116]. She somehow knew that God would understand her disillusionment.

The following morning, the open freight car which had been Lola and Daphne's home for ten days came to a sudden halt. This time they were ordered to disembark and began to walk towards an unknown destination.

---

[116] *Hebrew* A Jewish male (in Orthodox Judaism) is required to recite the Mourner's Kaddish after the death of a close relative, in order to help along the soul of the deceased in its journey upwards.

Chapter Six

(ii) *In Limbo*

Lola and Daphne stumbled along with all the other female prisoners, exhausted and freezing cold. Daphne suddenly collapsed and Lola bent down to help her up. It was her right leg. There was some kind of a spasm that most likely occurred because she had been motionless for so long. Daphne had no choice but to continue walking and she limped in excruciating pain. Lola took hold of Daphne's arm and helped her along.

After walking for some time, they were marched through huge iron gates. Lola knew that they had arrived at another camp and she wondered what evil awaited them. The women were then taken to their barracks. It was already crowded but Lola found a bed with one person on it and she sat on it with Daphne. The girl lying there was staring vacantly. For a moment Lola thought that she was dead but she moved her head to the side. Lola pushed the girl's legs to make room but she didn't react. Lola and Daphne settled onto the bunk and fell into a deep sleep.

Lola awoke suddenly in what seemed to be the middle of the night. She got up from the bed and walked to the door. She looked outside but there was no one around. As she ventured out, she realized that there weren't any guards on duty. Lola was desperate to have a shower so she went looking for a wash room. Lola saw another female prisoner walking towards her and Lola spoke to her in the limited German she had learnt at Birkenau.

"*Waschen, waschen*[117]," she said, moving her hands around in circles. The woman motioned for Lola to follow her. She went past Lola's barrack and turned the corner. She entered another barrack which had many tubs filled with water. The fellow prisoner picked up a bar of soap and handed it to Lola.

"*Danke*[118]," said Lola.

Her fellow prisoner smiled.

"Where are we?" asked Lola.

"Ravensbruck."

"Poland?"

"No, Germany," she replied before leaving.

Lola picked up a sponge which was beside one of the tubs and began washing herself. She washed herself twice in an attempt to get rid of the filth from her ten day train journey.

Feeling so much better after her wash, Lola crawled back onto her bunk and slept through the rest of the night. When Lola woke up the next morning, she felt extremely cold. She touched the girl beside her and she was frozen solid. She then touched Daphne's leg and thankfully it was warm. It felt so strange to get up in a leisurely way with no whistles and no one to push you or beat you. Some prisoners were wandering around

---

[117]*German* Wash, clean, sponge down.
[118]*German* Thank you.

the barrack while others were eating. She saw that people were lining up outside for soup so she woke Daphne and they joined the line for food. Once they had their bowls filled with soup, they were also given a piece of stale dark brown bread. They ate it all, enthusiastically.

After breakfast, Lola had to face the grim task of removing the corpse from their bunk and putting it outside on top of the pile of dead bodies. For Lola and Daphne, life carried on like this for the next few weeks. During the day, they would sit around listening to gossip. Ravensbruck was an all-women's camp and there were no kapos there. The SS guards seemed to avoid them. There was no *appell*[119] and no weekly selections. They were given soup twice a day, and they were allowed to wash in the tubs that Lola had discovered on her first night. There were constant rumours circulating that the Russians and Americans were approaching but all they could do was just sit and wait.

One morning, Lola awoke to the unlikely sound of birds tweeting. She realised that spring had arrived. Her moment of joy passed quickly as she looked at Daphne and saw sweat running down her face. Lola touched Daphne gently on the forehead. She was burning up with fever. Lola fetched a bowl of water and a sponge and began wiping her down. She tried to get her to come to the soup line but she was unable to stand. Lola risked her life by going into the soup line twice in order to bring a bowl to Daphne, who only managed a few small sips. She placed the bowl aside

---

[119]*German* Roll call.

and only during the evening she thought about having it herself but knew the risk. This continued for a few days but Daphne didn't seem to be improving at all. A girl from their barrack approached Lola.

"Let me examine your friend," she said.

"Are you a doctor?" asked Lola.

"Not quite," she replied, "I had one year to go before the Germans arrived in Poland."

This young looking, soft spoken girl was the daughter of a Rabbi from the Polish city of Wroclaw. She had also been in Auschwitz-Birkenau before being transported to Ravensbruck. Lola had never seen or met her until now. For the next week, the medical student from Wroclaw looked after Daphne, doing what she could under the circumstances. One morning Lola awoke to find Daphne shivering and hallucinating. She was muttering incomprehensibly. Lola called the medical student to come and attend to Daphne.

The girl intimated to Lola to prepare herself for the worst. Lola began to cry.

"Please, do something I've lost everyone. She's my best friend. We survived everything together."

The medical student held Lola's face and told her calmly, "Lola listen to me, whoever is not born, does not die. It's her time to go."

"Was it everyone else's time to go as well?" asked Lola.

The girl from Wroclaw knew what Lola meant.

She sat there in silence, not being able to give an answer. Instead, she placed her arm around Lola's shoulders and wept with her. The following

morning Lola awoke, shivering. She had felt that coldness before and she knew without doubt that her friend had passed away. Lola lay there, motionless. She did not touch Daphne's cold body nor did she raise her head to look at her. It wasn't until several hours later, when the medical student approached her bed, that Lola got up in a dazed state. Together they lifted Daphne's body and took it outside. They gently placed it on the pile of corpses. They went back inside the barrack and stood next to Daphne's bed. The Rabbi's daughter began to recite the Kaddish[120].
Less than a week after Daphne's death, for the first time since arriving in Ravensbruck, Lola's barrack was ordered to line up outside. A male SS guard signalled with his arm, dividing the group of prisoners in half. The group on the left were ordered to march towards the front of the camp. Lola who was in the other group watched as the medical student from Wroclaw left with the other women. It was the last time that Lola saw her. Lola was now all alone. Both of her friends were dead and the kind medical student had been taken away.

The rumours in the camp were rife. The women who were taken away were apparently moved to other camps. It was said that the rest of them would be sent away in the days to come. Lola did not know what to make of everything she heard; she just waited patiently.
April arrived and Lola sensed some sort of shift. The days were getting longer and sunnier. During the day she would sit on a bench in front of the

---

[120]*Hebrew* The mourner's prayer. A female is only allowed to recite the Kaddish if there are no males present.

barrack, soaking in the sun's rays. She would sit there for hours, sometimes until sunset.

As the end of April approached, the gunfire and explosions became louder. One day there were rumours that the Russians were 2 km away. The next day they were said to be 20 km away. No one really knew what was happening and there was a sense of apprehension and uncertainty amongst the prisoners. They knew that the SS would not abandon the camp and just leave them there. They would either kill them or take them somewhere else.

One morning a prisoner came rushing into Lola's barrack to share the news that there would be a selection just like there was in Auschwitz-Birkenau.

At first Lola found that hard to believe as she had been told that there were no gas chambers in Ravensbruck. After three months of being there, Lola was shocked to discover that there was one gas chamber at the camp.

It wasn't death that frightened her but she did not want to die in a gas chamber. The screams of the victims who were being gassed day and night at Auschwitz-Birkenau left an indelible mark that created deep psychological scars. Lola had decided that if it was her turn to die, she wanted to be shot.

Lola heard the dreaded whistle blow and everyone was ordered to line up outside. Lola expected to be told to undress but this selection was very different from the one at Auschwitz-Birkenau. They stood there dressed in their striped uniforms. Lola was in the third of four rows of prisoners.

A male SS guard approached them and looked closely at each prisoner. As he moved up and down the rows, he made eye contact with each one knowing that he had the power to determine if they lived or died. Tears rolled down Lola's cheeks. She knew that she was very lucky to still be alive but for the months spent in Ravensbruck they had no idea what would become of them and many, like Lola, had dared to be hopeful. Now, they feared the worst.

As the SS guard got closer to her, Lola wiped the tears from her face and stood completely motionless, staring straight ahead and avoiding eye contact. He took a very brief look at her and then he moved on. Once he had looked at all the prisoners he then started to point at them. Some of those chosen did not move and were dragged away by a female SS guard. The male guard then approached the third row and Lola's heart stood still. He walked past her and stopped at the end of the row where he pointed to another innocent soul.

As soon as the selection was over and the prisoners dismissed, Lola went straight to her bed. She began to sob and could not believe that once again she has been spared. The women who were selected were waiting outside. A whistle blew and they are ordered to start walking. Lola could hear their cries and screams as they marched away. Lola's heart was breaking to think that these girls had survived so much only to be gassed now at the eleventh hour.

Chapter Seven

From Despair to Joy

(i) The Death March

The following morning Lola awoke to the sound of a whistle. The women were ordered to hurry up and assemble outside the barrack. They were given a small piece of brown bread and, just like on their last day at Auschwitz-Birkenau, they were each given a blanket. Lola was sure that they were going on another long march.

They exited Ravensbruck just as the sun rose and they walked through the sharp, cold air. Lola slowly chewed on her piece of bread as she trudged along. Lola couldn't help but notice the vivid green of the trees along the way. As they walked she lost all track of time and exhaustion began to overcome her. They walked through a completely deserted village. Lola saw daffodils blooming in the gardens of the empty houses and knew for sure that it was spring. Soon after they had left the town, they found themselves in a forest where they were ordered to stop walking and to sit down. Lola still had a small piece of bread left and she ate it all not knowing if they would be given any more.

Lola and the other women slept on the forest ground and awoke to the chirping of birds. It was still dark and Lola wanted to sleep some more but the harsh voices of the SS guards rang out.

"Aufstehen, aufstehen[121]," they yelled.

The women reluctantly got up and started walking again. They were exhausted and hungry but were not given anything to eat. As they marched, they could hear the deafening sound of gunshots. Every prisoner that fell was immediately shot. Lola willed herself to keep walking. She did not want to die there, anonymously in a strange and unknown place. Lola turned to the female prisoner beside her, "*Germania*[122]?" she asked.

The young girl nodded wearily.

The second day of the march was worse than the first. They were all walking on empty stomachs and completely exhausted. Many were coughing. Many were dropping to the ground and they were immediately shot.

Lola tried her best to ignore the sound of gunshots and never looked back at who had been shot in case she knew the victim personally. Lola could not even stop to relieve herself as that would have been a death sentence.

As evening approached, the prisoners were ordered to stop next to a huge barn. The SS guards approached the farmer in the barn. After an exchange of words, the farmer left the barn. As he walked away he glanced at the female prisoners and was clearly shocked by what he saw.

The women entered the barn and made their way to the piles of straw that were scattered throughout the barn. Lola sat down and although it was just straw it felt like the most comfortable bed. As she lay down she became

---

[121]**Get up.**
[122]***Greek* Germany**

acutely aware of her hunger and thirst. Lola stood up and went to the door of the barn. She was not sure why or what she was looking for. She looked through a gap in the door and saw the SS guards smoking and chatting. She despised them with every fibre of her being. She just wanted to survive to see them pay for their crimes. She turned and went back to her makeshift bed in the hay. The barn was completely silent. Everyone was so exhausted that they had fallen asleep as soon as they had settled in the straw. Lola closed her eyes and tried to think of better days to come before falling into a deep sleep.

As usual, the shouts of the guards woke them in the morning. Lola stood up and she realized that the girl beside her was motionless. Her face had turned grey and she was stiff and frozen to Lola's touch. Sadly, Lola was getting used to waking up next to corpses. They made their way outside and surprisingly they were each given a piece of bread. Lola took a tiny nibble of the bread, chewing slowly and deliberately. In this way, she made the small ration last a long time. Lola was desperately thirsty but they were not given any water. Lola did not know how much longer she would be able to go on like this. At sunset, the prisoners were led into a forest and told to sit. When the women were told to get up the next morning, many of them stayed on the ground, too exhausted to move. The male SS guard yelled at them to get up and if they did not obey, he shot them in the head.

They resumed the march without any food. As they trudged along, they heard gunfire and loud explosions in the distance. Lola could see that the

SS guards looked perturbed as they spoke amongst themselves. A female SS guard walked up alongside Lola.

"Don't call me *Aufseherin*[123] anymore," said the female SS guard to Lola, "From now on call me by my name, Gerda."

Lola nodded as the guard moved on to the prisoner in front. Lola knew that she had to obey the guard call her anything she wanted for she still had the power. Lola quickly realised the significance of the guard not wanting to be addressed by her official title. Normally, prisoners would be shot for not using the correct title. Lola knew it must be a matter of days before this long nightmare came to an end. All she had to do was to hold on and be strong for a little while longer. That night they slept in the forest again but there was a different feeling in the air. The gunfire and mortar explosions were closer and the SS guards looked worried.

The following morning they were awoken by a huge explosion. They were ordered to get up quickly and the SS began marching them in the direction they had come from the day before. A few hours later they were told to take a rest. This was strange since they had never taken a rest after such a short time. Lola was convinced it was because of the bombardments that were being heard all around them. Lola sat down next to the other female prisoners. Suddenly, without warning, the male SS guards began firing at the prisoners. There was panic and screaming and many of the girls began running away. Lola jumped up and began to run as well. She didn't know

---

[123] *German* During the Second World War, the SS female guards were given this title, which means female overseer.

where she was running to, she simply followed the others. The girl in front of her was shot and fell to the ground but Lola continued to run as fast as she could. The group of girls ran and ran until they came to a road. They could see a huge tank coming towards them and they ran back into the forest believing it was a German tank. There were soldiers next to the tank and they followed the girls, shouting out in a foreign language. Some of the prisoners who understood the language ran back and hugged the soldiers.

"They're Russian soldiers," said one prisoner.

Lola stood there in disbelief, unable to comprehend that she had finally been liberated.

Chapter Seven

(ii) Bittersweet Freedom

The next few hours were surreal for Lola. The 'death march' survivors trustingly followed their Russian saviours. The Russian soldiers stared at the women with pity and in disbelief. Lola found herself walking again but this time it was different. She felt full of energy even though she was starving and exhausted. She felt the wonderful freedom of not having to worry about being shot at or killed. Lola delighted in the fact that the Germans had finally lost the war. She felt a sense of satisfaction to see them down on their knees. At one point, they passed a large field dotted with many people just sitting on the ground. As they got closer, Lola saw that they were German soldiers who were now Prisoners of War. Eventually, Lola's group was led into what appeared to be a Nazi concentration camp that had been taken over by the Russians. They were taken to the barracks where they were free to rest. Lola found an empty bed and she slept for the rest of the day and right through the night. When she awoke in the morning, she could still not believe that she was finally free.

"Come," said one of the women, "They're serving breakfast."

Lola went outside and joined a line of male and female survivors in front of another barrack. Once inside the building, she was handed a bowl of soup with a thick piece of white bread. At the end of the queue she was given a small plate with a piece of cake on it and a cup of some kind of hot beverage. Lola was completely shocked and overwhelmed at the sight of this food. She excitedly sat at one of the tables. The first thing she did was to take a sip of the hot drink. To her utter amazement, she realized that it was hot cocoa. She had not had this since Salonica. She relished every morsel of food and drink as she silently thanked God over and over again. Breakfast lasted for well over an hour as everyone was eating slowly. Once Lola was finished her meal, she went to the wash rooms with some of the girls whom she knew from Ravensbruck. There were ten shower heads hanging from the ceiling, just like the sauna at Auschwitz-Birkenau. This time however there was no time limit, and Lola and the other girls stayed under that water for as long as they wanted.

For the first time, since Lola had arrived in Auschwitz, she was given normal clothes to wear. With great satisfaction, they all threw the striped prisoner's uniforms into the fire. The girls had a huge pile of women's clothes to choose from which had undoubtedly belonged to Jewish victims but no one spoke of it. Once they were dressed, the girls decided to walk to the nearest village. No one knew where they were in Germany but they did not care.

When they reached the village they saw former camp prisoners, who were still wearing their striped uniforms, walking in and out of the stores along the main street. As they approached they were told that no one was around. The prisoners, with help from some Soviet soldiers, broke the windows of the stores and began looting whatever they could carry. The girls just stood there not knowing what to do. A former male camp prisoner approached them saying, "Go for it girls, take whatever you want."

There was a man standing in the middle of the road handing out pretzels that he had apparently found in the back room of a bakery. Lola couldn't resist. She took a pretzel and began eating it slowly. It took her the entire day to finish it. Another man approached the girls handing out watches and jewellery. Lola received a beautiful watch with a round face and a thick silver band.

"That's a man's watch," said one of the girls.

Lola didn't care. She put it on and remembered her own watch which was taken from her upon her arrival at Auschwitz-Birkenau.

That evening they were once again served a substantial meal which consisted of a thick soup with plenty of potatoes and carrots, a thick piece of white bread, a small piece of chocolate cake and a bar of chocolate which the Russians handed out. After dinner as Lola made her way back to her barrack, a Russian soldier grabbed her arm, trying to pull her watch off. She pulled back and yelled, "Oxi."[124]

A Russian officer approached them and asked what was going on. Lola pointed to her watch and then pointed to the soldier, indicating that he wanted to take it. Lola did not speak Russian but she knew from the tone of the Officer that he was scolding the soldier.

The next morning Lola was up early and was one of the first to be served a simple but nourishing breakfast. Even though it wasn't much, it felt like a

---

[124] *Greek* No.

feast. After breakfast, Lola went for a long walk with some of the girls. It was springtime and the flowers were in full bloom. It was a joy to walk down the street in such fine weather, as a free woman. One of the girls had taken a blanket and when they arrived at the edge of the forest, they placed the blanket down on the ground and sat down to rest. They each took out of their pockets the chocolate bar which they had saved from the night before. As they slowly ate and talked, Lola was asked a question which she hadn't thought about since leaving Salonica.

"How old are you?" asked one of the girls.

Lola looked away for a moment, she had honestly forgotten.

"I was born in 1926," she said.

"So you're nineteen years old."

"Yes," said Lola, "I believe I am."

Later that day, back at the camp, Lola lay on her bed and was deep in thought. She thought about how different she was as a sixteen year old prior to being deported. So much had happened, so much had changed. Lola realised that she would never be the same person as that innocent sixteen year old girl.

That evening as Lola walked back to her barrack after dinner, she was approached by the Russian soldier who had harassed her the previous night. There was no one around and Lola felt afraid. He waved his pistol at her and said something in Russian. Lola knew that he wanted the watch. She was not going to have an argument with someone who was pointing a gun at her. She removed the watch and handed it over to him. That night she cried herself to sleep.

Two weeks later, the Russians announced that they were going to organise to send people back to their countries of birth. Lola was in a dilemma. She assumed that her sister Rachel was still alive in Salonica but she did not want to go back to Greece. Besides Rachel, Lola's immediate family and most of her extended family had been murdered by the Nazis. She felt that she wanted to go to another country, to start anew and then she could send for her sister. Two of the girls that she had become friendly with were from Belgium. They had been deported to Auschwitz-Birkenau in 1943 but it was in Ravensbruck that Lola had met them. They told her to say that she was from Belgium and they helped her fill in a form that they had been given.

In mid-May, all of the survivors who claimed to be from Western Europe were finally being moved elsewhere. They boarded a large truck and waved at the Russian soldiers as the truck departed. It was a very short drive, perhaps not more than an hour, when they arrived at what seemed like another camp. Foreign looking soldiers helped them get off the trucks. "Look up there," said Lola's friend excitedly, "It's the American flag." They had arrived at Ludwigslust, ten miles from where they had been. The Americans were in charge and had taken over a former Nazi labour camp. This was to be Lola's home for the next month. Lola found the conditions at this camp were much better than at the Russian camp. There was more food and every week each person would be examined by a doctor. During one of these examinations, the American doctor spoke to Lola in a foreign language that Lola had heard in the camps.

"*Zeneniridishe*[125]?" he asked.

Lola didn't understand so she ignored him. The girl behind her who was from Poland told her in broken German, which Lola had learnt in Auschwitz-Birkenau, that the doctor was speaking in Yiddish and that he was asking if she was Jewish.

"*Nein*[126]," replied Lola.

"Don't worry," said the girl next to her, "You can tell the truth. The doctor is also a Jew."

Lola then nodded and the doctor gave her a smile.

Approximately, a month later, there was news that the Americans would be leaving the area as the Soviet Army was taking over. They began transporting all refugees into the American zone[127] which was further south. Lola, claiming to be from Belgium, was transported out of Ludwigslust in late June. Once more, with her Belgian friends, they boarded an army truck and headed south-west to an unknown destination. As Lola sat in the truck, she felt that spiritually she was moving further and further away from Auschwitz-Birkenau and Ravensbruck. Tears filled her eyes as she thought about Daphne and Eutixia. For the first time she

---

[125] *Yiddish* Are you Jewish?
[126] *German* No
[127] At the end of the Second World War the four Allied powers divided Germany into four occupation zones. The American zone consisted of territory in the south and western part of the country.

felt she was able to mourn her family and her two close friends who had lost their lives in hell itself.

Even though Lola was overjoyed to finally be free, she constantly thought about all of the atrocities that had repeatedly occurred in the camps. One of the things that haunted her over and over was the murder of at least five of the girls who worked with her in Kanada. After having survived for so long together, they were gunned down by the SS guards minutes before they were liberated by the Russians. Lola was never able to come to terms with this injustice.

Chapter Eight

New Dreams

The US army truck that was carrying the displaced persons from Ludwigslust had been travelling for a few hours. Lola sat at the window and was looking out as the truck passed through town after town. She tried to read the name of the towns as they drove by. One of those signs displayed the name 'Kassel'[128] with an arrow pointing to the right. A short while later they had arrived at their destination. Everyone got off the truck and were greeted by American soldiers. Lola noticed that they appeared to be so pleasant and easy going. Lola and her group were asked to follow an American woman who led them to their sleeping quarters. The women were separated from the men. The room had a line of beds on both sides and it looked somewhat like a hospital ward. A few of the beds were already occupied. Lola was shown to her bed and for a moment she thought she may be dreaming as the bed had a mattress with clean sheets, a blanket and a pillow. She couldn't believe it and was so overcome with emotion that she wanted to cry. Lola was emotionally numb by this stage and the tears did not come. Someone came and placed some linen on Lola's bed. She carefully unfolded them and found a bath towel, a face towel and a pink night dress. She picked up the nightdress and held it to

---

[128] The city of Kassel is located in northern Hesse, which is a region in western Germany.

her face. It smelled so clean and it reminded her of her own pretty night dresses back in Salonica. Lola's mind jumped back to her first night at Auschwitz-Birkenau. She thought of the horrors of that camp and how different it was to now be treated as a human being.

The new arrivals were shown around the camp which would be their new home until they could be relocated. They were told that they were in the town of Kassel and their Displaced Persons camp was a former Nazi Labour camp. The Americans and the International Red Cross had transformed it into a makeshift DP[129] camp.

That evening at dinner time, Lola ate meat for the first time in four and a half years. Even before Greece entered the war in 1940, her family could not buy meat. Lola remembers thinking that the taste and texture of it was as wondrous as a *loukoumi*[130]. The roasted potatoes and the vegetables were served with a delicious tasting gravy that she had never had before. The meal was like *manna*[131] from heaven. For dessert, each person was given a small tin of sweetened apple conserve. As Lola ate, she thought of her father and his tin making factory back home. She suddenly got a lump in her throat as so many emotions welled up in her.

---

[129] A DP camp is a temporary facility for displaced persons and/or refugees. The term is mainly used for camps established after the Second World War in central Europe.

[130] *Greek* A fragrant sweet cube of jelly that is heavily dusted with icing sugar, which is also known as Turkish delight. In Greek, the word 'loukoumi' is used as an adjective to describe foodstuff as 'delicious'.

[131] In the Old Testament, 'manna' is the food that was miraculously supplied to the Israelites in their journey through the wilderness.

After dinner, Lola went to her bed where she found a toothbrush, toothpaste and a comb. Once again she was taken aback at this wonderful surprise. This was a day that she would never forget.

For the next three months Lola continued to keep company with the girls from Belgium whom she had met in Ravensbruck. Whenever they were given a pass, they would go into the nearest town and window shop. They stared at the latest fashions and dreamed of being able to start their lives over again.

One sunny day as they walked along the main street of a local town, one of the girls asked another girl, "Why are you wearing your cardigan? It's so warm."

"Because she's embarrassed of the tattooed number on her arm," replied another girl.

In broken German Lola stepped in, "Leave her alone! Some of us are embarrassed of the tattoo and some of us aren't. She must do what makes her feel comfortable."

"She shouldn't feel embarrassed…"

"I feel embarrassed," said Lola, "That's why I always have my left arm in a position so that no one can see my tattooed number."

"Is it because you don't want others to see your tattoo or is it because you don't want to look at it?"

"Both," replied Lola.

The girls continued walking in silence. They never discussed their permanent pale-blue scars again.

For the rest of the summer Lola and her friends made the most of their newly found freedom. They created a schedule to keep themselves busy. Three times a week they would venture into town and on one of those days they would go to the local cinema. They had no money but they did receive movie vouchers from the DP camp. Every Sunday afternoon they would watch an American movie. Unable to read the German subtitles, Lola remembers these days as her introduction to the English language. They were her first English lessons.

One morning in early September, Lola was combing her hair and one of her friends kept staring at her.
"Your hair has grown," she said.
Lola smiled.
"Mine hasn't," the friend said as she touched her hair, "It's still very short and I can't do anything with it."
"Don't worry it will grow," said Lola.
"But yours has grown so fast."
"That's because I'm Greek-Spanish," she said jokingly, "We have a lot of hair."

In that same month many changes began to take place in the DP camp. At this time, Lola had a vivid dream - one that she would never forget. She dreamt of the White Tower of Salonica. It had been two and a half years since she had last dreamt that the tower had completely collapsed. In her new dream however, she was walking along Nikis Avenue the White

Tower was as round as ever and standing tall. The day after that dream, the entire camp was summoned to a meeting after breakfast. Lola and her friends made their way to a big empty hall. They sat towards the front and within a few minutes it was completely full. An American military official took to the stage and spoke in German. Another American soldier translated every sentence into French. Lola could not understand what was being said. Her mind wandered off and she thought of Daphne who was the best interpreter. Lola knew exactly what was happening in Auschwitz-Birkenau because Daphne spoke French and German. She missed her friend so deeply. After the meeting, Lola asked her friends to explain what was going on.

"Certain countries like Belgium won't accept the refugees that have no papers," explained one of the Belgian girls.

"But if it's your country how can they deny you entry?" asked Lola.

"In our case, they will look at the birth registrar's office and they should find our names there."

"Does that mean I can't go to Belgium?" asked Lola.

"I think so," replied the Belgian girl, "Unless you have a relative there who is willing to sponsor you. But don't worry about it because tomorrow we will learn more when they give us a form to fill in."

That evening all Lola did was worry. She couldn't believe that she wouldn't be able to get into Belgium. She had no papers or any relatives in Belgium. Perhaps her only option now was to go back to Salonica to try to find her sister. The thought of going back to her own country without her parents caused her great emotional pain. She truly did not know what to do.

The following day they were all given a form to fill in. She took the form and went outside. She sat at a bench feeling helpless and forlorn. Lola had put all her hope into going to Belgium and now she knew she would not be allowed in. She began to cry. Then, out of nowhere, a man appeared.

"Hello do you remember me? I am Gerard" he asked in German.

"No," replied Lola.

"Didn't you work in Kanada at Auschwitz-Birkenau?" asked the man.

"Yes I did."

"I remember you, because you gave me a loaf of bread when I needed it most."

Lola instantly remembered the event but the man was unrecognisable. One day when Lola was in the sauna building waiting to take a shower, a male prisoner who worked there begged her for a loaf of bread. He told her that he had heard that the workers in Kanada received extra food. This was not altogether true as it was not a regular occurrence. The man went on to say that his sixteen year old son was very weak and ill and desperately needed solid food. Lola remembered saying to the man, "I'll see what I can do. After the shower follow me to the warehouse."

When Lola returned to her block, she approached Daphne and told her of the man's request. Lola begged Daphne to help as she felt a strong need to help this man and his son. Daphne spoke to the Czech woman who then approached Lola and said she should follow her. They left the warehouse and the man who was waiting outside went with them. They entered another block where the Czech woman reached into a box and pulled out two loaves of bread and handed them to Lola.

Lola thanked her profusely and went outside to where Gerard was waiting. She handed him both of the loaves, even though she knew that one of the loaves was intended for her. Gerard kissed her hand and told her he would never forget her.

As Lola sat on the bench at the DP camp remembering the situation, she asked him, "How is your son?"

"He died," replied Gerard.

"I'm so sorry," said Lola.

"You were the only person to ever help me at my most desperate moment," said Gerard.

Lola smiled at him.

"Tell me, why are you crying?" he asked.

When Lola finished explaining her predicament, he said to her, "Now it's my turn to help you."

"But how can you help me?" asked Lola.

"Firstly, I'm Belgian," he replied, "Secondly, I will tell the authorities that you are my cousin. I will get you through."

Lola could not believe her good fortune. He filled out their forms and handed them in, hoping for the best outcome.

During the next month, Lola attended two weddings at the DP camp. The camp was filled with so many young Jewish men and women from all over Europe who were all alone in the world as their entire families had been annihilated. The weddings took place in the main hall of the camp.

Afterwards, everyone was given a piece of cake which the Americans provided. Before the weddings, Lola helped with the setting up of the chuppah[132]. It was impossible to find prayer shawls to cover the canopy. Someone suggested that they collect the table cloths from the dining room and sew them together to create a canopy. Lola was assigned to gather the table cloths, which she did without permission from the Americans. One of the women was a seamstress and she created a beautiful chuppah out of three tablecloths.

In early October all of the Belgian nationals in the DP camp received official papers that would enable them to go back to their country. Gerard rushed to find Lola the minute he received his papers.

"I told them that despite being a Greek national you will come with me to Belgium because you are my cousin," he said.

Lola was so thankful and excited that she finally had permission to go to Belgium despite it being under false pretences. They departed from the DP camp in mid-October. They were taken in a truck to the main railway station in Kassel which brought back harrowing memories for most of the refugees. However, once they boarded a passenger train, they finally felt safe and relieved to once again be living a civilised life. Lola sat on the train next to her 'cousin' and it didn't take long before she fell asleep. She was awoken by the sound of a whistle.

"We've arrived in Brussels," said Gerard.

---

[132] *Hebrew* A canopy under which a Jewish couple stand during their wedding ceremony.

They made their way to customs and they were told that Lola could enter Belgium but that she had to go immediately to the Greek Embassy and ask for their help. Once in the waiting room, there was an announcement that all refugees who were not Belgian citizens had to board a bus which was waiting outside. Lola and Gerard said their goodbyes and he gave Lola a piece of paper with an address on it.

"Come and visit me whenever you're ready," he said.

As Lola walked off she turned around once more and waved at him. She boarded the bus, unsure of what awaited her. Half an hour later the bus stopped outside the Italian Embassy which Lola recognized because of the Italian flag. Two names were called out and they quickly exited the bus. This was followed by a few other Embassy stops before the bus stopped at the Greek Embassy. Lola's name was the only one called out. She got off the bus and stood still for a moment staring at the Greek flag. It was a bittersweet moment for her because finally she felt safe but very sad as she believed she might be the only member of her entire family to have survived the carnage of the past two and a half years.

One evening as she wandered through the inner city streets of Brussels, a well-dressed gentleman approached her and asked if she needed any help, for she appeared to be lost. She told him that she had been in a concentration camp and that she had lost all her family and was alone in the world. She explained how the Greek Embassy in Brussels had placed her at a boarding house which was run by the Belgian Red Cross. She had no way of knowing that this kind gentleman was also Jewish. He invited her to his home where his wife gave her a meal, drew a bath for her, and invited her to stay in their spare bedroom. The following morning they told her that they were also Jewish and that they would sponsor her. That same morning they informed the Greek Embassy that Lola was now legally sponsored to stay in Belgium.

Determined to stand on her own two feet, Lola insisted on working for the couple in return for food and shelter. Every morning she ground the coffee beans, brewed the coffee, cleared the breakfast table and then cleaned the house. She was so grateful to find herself in this position that on one day when she was alone, she embraced the feather duster that she was holding and thanked God in an impromptu prayer. She was just happy to be with people who were kind to her.

Slowly but surely the dice began to roll in Lola's favour. Within a period of three months, she experienced what she says were two miracles.

The first miracle was meeting her beloved husband. She had been living at the Belgian couple's home for six months, when their handsome nephew Morris, a survivor of the Buchenwald concentration camp, came to live with them. For Lola it was love at first sight. Not only was this man tall and handsome but he was also a wonderful human being, full of kindness, sensitivity and respect. Not even two months had passed when one Sunday afternoon the handsome and debonair Morris proposed to Lola on bended knee, offering her an exquisite, sparkling engagement ring. How bittersweet this moment was for Lola. One of the happiest days of her life but no family to share it with.

Although Lola had been raised in an Orthodox Jewish family, she preferred not to have the religious ceremony. Memories of her family, all murdered in Auschwitz, would have spoiled the day for her. The civil marriage ceremony took place at the registry office in downtown Brussels. Lola was dressed in a navy blue suit with a white flower in her hair and a bouquet of white lilies. There wasn't anything that could dampen her spirits that day.

Precisely a week after her wedding day, the second miracle occurred. She received a letter from the International Red Cross informing her that her sister Rachel, who had spent the duration of the war in hiding, was now searching for her family who had been deported in 1943. As Lola read the letter, her hands began trembling. No amount of words could describe the feeling of joy that she felt the moment she realised that she had finally located her Rachel who was still living in Salonica.

Brussels, Belgium
May 1, 1947

Lola gazed at her left arm. The pale-blue tattoo was a permanent part of her now, so all she could do was to try to keep it hidden. Although a vain woman by nature, this was not the reason for wanting to hide the five digit number that had not only scarred her youthful arm but had also left an indelible scar on her mind. She looked at it every day. The number 39403 had replaced her name for two years and was now her constant companion. After everything that she had been through, she was sentenced to never forgetting the horrors that she had experienced, every time she glanced at her left arm. The only way to try to block out the constant reminder was to keep her arm covered at all times

Lola looked at the dusty pink dress that was on her bed. The seamstress had shortened the sleeves to three quarter length, but the first two digits of the tattooed number were still visible. Lola immediately returned the dress to have it altered. In three days, she was leaving for Australia, where her husband had established himself a year before. She had prepared everything and could not wait to join him in the 'land of milk and honey'. This was the name he had given to Australia in all of his letters to Lola.

Brussels, Belgium
May 4, 1947

Lola was in her room preparing for her departure to Australia to join her husband. The sound of a May Day Parade on the streets of Brussels floated up through Lola's window and her mind was transported back to the very last school parade that she had attended in Salonica, Greece. It was only seven years ago, when she was a naïve fourteen year old girl. So much had happened, so much had changed. She and everything around her would never be the same again.

"My Salonica, my Salonica," she muttered under her breath, as tears welled up in her eyes. She closed her eyes as she thought back to that picture perfect day in March 1940.

Lola couldn't stop the memories from flooding back. She thought about her beloved parents. Righteous and noble, that's how she remembered them. Her mother was a tall, statuesque woman with sandy blonde hair. She was undoubtedly the most beautiful of all mothers, in Lola's eyes.

There was a knock on Lola's bedroom door. She heard Morris's aunt call out to her.

"Lola, are you awake? We're leaving in two hours."

"Thank you," said Lola, "I'll be ready."

Lola was soon ready to depart for the next big adventure of her life. He parents-in-law took her to the central railway station where she boarded a train for Marseilles, France. From there she boarded the ship that took her to Australia.

Australia

And so it was, far away from Europe, that Lola began her brand new life. She and her husband would run a successful bakery and raise a son and daughter.

Five years later, in 1952, Lola and her husband sponsored Lola's sister, now known as Maria, and her English husband, to come and live in Melbourne.

The two sisters had not seen each other in nine years. They were both forever changed but their sisterly bond was strong. They were never separated again and despite all their past sufferings, they tried to remain positive and focused on the future. They were determined more than ever to make the most of every single day.

Lola's tranquil, happy existence in Australia was a far cry from what she had been so cruelly forced to endure during the Holocaust.

Lola often says, "During my life, I had the misfortune to live in a place called hell but I have also been blessed to have experienced heaven."

POSTSCRIPT

Maria and George settled in to life in Melbourne. For Maria, it meant everything to her to be close to her sister Lola.

In 1954, Maria gave birth to a baby girl called Margaret. George was keen to return to England to introduce Margaret to his family. Maria did not want to leave Melbourne but in 1955, at her husband's insistence, they went back to England.

A year later, in 1956, Margaret contracted meningitis and died in the hospital in Portsmouth, England. In 1957, a heartbroken Maria and her husband returned to Melbourne.

George and Maria bought a house in Ormond. They did not have any more children.

In 1961 Maria began working at a delicatessen at the Prahran market. Maria became an invaluable employee. Her fluency in Greek was very useful as she served the countless Greek customers until her retirement in 1992.

George died of lung cancer in 1999.

Lola was happily married to Morris until his death in 1989.

In 2010, Maria moved into Lola's house that she shared with her partner, Gary. For quite some time, Maria would go back to her own house every weekend.

Gary passed away in 2016 and Maria moved in permanently with Lola.

Maria passed away on October 6th, 2018. She is deeply missed by Lola and all who knew and loved her.

Lola is lucky to live close to her son and daughter and their families. Lola has five grandchildren and five great grandchildren.

Lola is still going strong and is ninety nine years old at the time of writing this book.

www.ingramcontent.com/pod-product-compliance
Lightning Source LLC
Chambersburg PA
CBHW061428300426
44114CB00014B/1590